Model Making

Model Making

Megan Werner

Princeton Architectural Press, New York

Published by
Princeton Architectural Press
37 East 7th Street
New York, NY 10003

Visit our website at www.papress.com

Editor: Nicola Bednarek Brower
Designer: Paul Wagner

Special thanks to:
Bree Anne Apperley, Sara Bader, Janet Behning,
Megan Carey, Carina Cha, Tom Cho, Penny (Yuen Pik) Chu,
Russell Fernandez, Jan Haux, Linda Lee, John Myers,
Katharine Myers, Dan Simon, Andrew Stepanian,
Jennifer Thompson, Joseph Weston, and Deb Wood of
Princeton Architectural Press
—Kevin C. Lippert, publisher

Library of Congress Cataloging-in-Publication Data
Werner, Megan.
Model making / Megan Werner.
159 p. : ill. (chiefly col.) ; 22 cm.
Includes bibliographical references.
ISBN 978-1-56898-870-2 (alk. paper)
1. Architectural models. I. Title.
NA2790.W47 2011
720.28—dc22
                              2010052061

The Architecture Brief Series takes on a variety of single topics of interest to architecture students and young professionals. Field-specific information and digital techniques are presented in a user-friendly manner along with basic principles of design and construction. The series familiarizes readers with the concepts and technical terms necessary to successfully translate ideas into built form.

Other titles in this series:

Architects Draw
Sue Ferguson Gussow
978-1-56898-740-8

Architectural Lighting:
Designing with Light and Space
Hervé Descottes
978-1-56898-938-9

Architectural Photography the Digital Way
Gerry Kopelow
978-1-56898-697-5

Building Envelopes:
An Integrated Approach
Jenny Lovell
978-1-56898-818-4

Digital Fabrications:
Architectural and Material Techniques
Lisa Iwamoto
978-1-56898-790-3

Ethics for Architects:
50 Dilemmas of Professional Practice
Thomas Fisher
978-1-56898-946-4

Material Strategies:
Innovative Applications in Architecture
Blaine Brownell
978-1-56898-986-0

Old Buildings, New Designs:
Architectural Transformations
Charles Bloszies
978-1-61689-035-3

Philosophy for Architects
Branko Mitrović
978-1-56898-994-5

Sustainable Design:
A Critical Guide
David Bergman
978-1-56898-941-9

Urban Composition:
Developing Community through Design
Mark C. Childs
978-1-61689-052-0

Writing about Architecture:
Mastering the Language of Buildings and Cities
Alexandra Lange
978-1-61689-053-7

Contents

Foreword

Emily Abruzzo

Having kindly given over their basement for so many years to the storage of the paper, wood, acrylic, plaster, and metal remnants of my education as a young architect, a few years ago my parents suggested that I take a look at my old models to see if any of them could "go." I had no hesitation about throwing the models away: most of them had been photographed, I was already in graduate school, and disposing of them would be, I thought, cathartic. No longer proud of that early, naive work that had at first given me such delight, I was glad to see it go, now fully invested in digital modeling. I brought the models out to the curb and piled them up for garbage collection.

After a night of heavy rain, a mess of wet cardboard and rusty metal was all that was left the next morning. What were the previous day useless objects taking up space, embarrassing reminders of work I no longer liked, had now been melted by the onslaught of weather. The cardboard slumped, twisted, and bowed, the soft woods curved and delaminated, paints peeled, and plaster crumbled. I was amazed not only by what I saw—I had thought these to be heartier objects—but also by my complex, conflicted emotions regarding these rejected works: it made me sad, disappointed, regretful to see them in such a state.

Of course, this destruction would have occurred regardless of the weather, but seeing that melted pile has, for me, made all the difference: it made me realize the intrinsic quality of models that I believe to be so important, and that is their ability to elicit emotion. While my regret was undoubtedly related to some remaining investment in my own work, it points to a larger truth: that, nearly always, designers, clients, or others who encounter and interact with models form a connection with them.

A physical model is the material embodiment of an idea, and therein lies its magic. By becoming real, it gives life and actuality to an idea in a way that two-dimensional expressions rarely can. While a drawing might prefer, for example, a specific angle of view, the model often has no such luxury. With its three-dimensionality, its reaction to light and materiality, a model is perceived in innumerable and unpredictable ways. The viewer's active role—the onus to construct view, to place one's eye and hand on the object, and take in its space, details, shape, or texture—allows for an emotional relationship, a guttural connection, a feeling of investment and perhaps even authorship.

While models might be seen as the most rational of all forms of architectural communication (simply, a building in miniature or a detail at full scale), they hardly seem to belong to a rationalized system. Unlike drawing, where the language of projections, the surreal flatness of the elevation, and the concept of the section are separations from reality that must be learned in order to be understood, the model does not require abstract methodologies for its comprehension. It is intuitive and liberated from over-rationalization, comprehended by the senses before it is interpreted by the brain. Models, it has been said, are real, and for this reason they communicate so well to so many.[1] This is why clients take such delight in them, why they convey the sense of a project even when drawings do not. This is why they are often the denouement of architects' presentations, and why students take such pride in them.

My first job, building models by hand for Peter Eisenman, began a trajectory with model making that is somewhat of a shared experience for architects of my generation. I was a crack model maker at the end of that summer, but quickly put aside these skills as I entered graduate school and spent more time computer modeling than making actual things. Over the course of the next few years, model making became scarce in my learning and work: even though I discarded very little after that eye-opening purge, only a few student models remain.

Of late, however, model making has experienced a kind of reverse bell curve. Once a mandatory part of the design process, it saw a rapid decline as computer modeling—though arguably a two-dimensional form of representation—came to replace physical models. But as quickly as we saw this decline, we have seen a reinvestment in making. While we are indeed more reliant on the computer than ever, this reversal is a result of the increasing ease of translating information created with the computer to reality through the use of digital fabrication techniques.

As modeling and fabrication come closer together, more models are being made, and, despite less hand production, the process might be more engaging than ever. Rapid prototyping technologies short-circuit the design process: the model is no longer necessarily referential, and its role more often now better described by the term *prototype*. Even when not working at full scale, it seems useful that the tools that make the model could be the ones used for the final object, piece, or pattern.

But better yet, as these new tools allow fast and accurate iterative production with ease, our emotions take an active role in the design process, helping to guide, along with objective information, each successive iteration. Models elicit gut reactions—you know what is right when you see it in front of you—and this reaction, or emotion, should be the most important tool used by every designer. The structural engineer Cecil Balmond has spoken about using intuition in design—the idea that as you learn, see, feel, and try, you develop a kind of internal sounding board that informs that gut reaction.[2] Models, especially when they come in greater numbers, are a useful design tool in that sense. While it is true that they can be very communicative to an audience—eliciting dreams, giving sensation, and engendering pleasure—they can speak volumes to the designer as well, if only he or she allows for the emotional.

In Scott Hicks's documentary *Glass: A Portrait of Philip in Twelve Parts* (2007), Philip Glass speaks about the difference between writing and hearing his symphonies. In writing, one must imagine how an entire orchestra will sound when playing the piece, and so the live performance is always revealing of something unexpected, even for an experienced composer like Glass.

In architecture, especially given contemporary technologies, we have the opportunity to test our compositions, to train our ear, as it were.

With typical drawing or computer modeling, your brain must interpolate that third dimension so critical to form, space, and the *je ne sais quoi* that makes design sing. But with rapid prototyping, we have the ability to make actual material objects, to full scale even, that approach the designer's equivalent of the full orchestra.

Like the symphony played live, the model, as an actual object in three dimensions, becomes an autonomous thing that one can hear, feel, or see for what it is. Freed from the work of having to invent a missing orchestra, or dimension, the brain is allowed to observe, analyze, and project. What do I see, is it successful, and, perhaps most importantly, how does it make me feel?

Notes

1   Olafur Eliasson, "Models are Real," in *Models, 306090 11,* ed. Emily Abruzzo and Jonathan Solomon (New York: 306090 Books, 2007).
2   Cecil Balmond and Eric Ellingsen, "Survival Patterns," in *Models, 306090 11, ed.* Emily Abruzzo and Jonathan Solomon (New York: 306090 Books, 2007).

Preface

Why build a model out of wood, acrylic, or metal, when you can render it digitally with remarkable realism? What is there to be gained from this ancient craft? In this book I hope to give readers not only a better understanding of the value of models—for the designer, the designer's audience, and model makers themselves—but to inspire in them a passion for the physical and intellectual pleasures of the craft, a love of making.

While many architecture students and young practitioners know models mainly as a challenging and time-consuming task to be fulfilled after the design process is completed, models are in fact first and foremost a means for investigation, for carrying an idea forward. As such, physical models are a uniquely revealing and compelling tool. More forcefully than any other way of visualizing a building—apart from its actual construction—models represent ideas, as opposed to images. Embedded in the model is the concept of the design, which the model translates into matter and time. And each of these worlds—the material and the temporal—imposes itself on the designer's investigation. Physical models make the invisible visible: the rules that apply to matter and time become evident to the model maker and thus become filters for his or her design explorations. Suddenly, the designer is faced with both the limitations of the material and its opportunities in the real world.

Imagine, for example, exploring an idea about a cylindrical building element. As long as you are merely thinking about or drawing it, it is simply a geometrical form. Once you build it in physical space, however, it must be a rubber cylinder, a tiny cylinder, a rigid cylinder, an opaque cylinder, a smooth cylinder, or a rough one. In other words, you have to commit to many other qualities beyond the geometry.

And yet, while requiring such decisions, the model does not demand particular ones, allowing for exploration. However tangible, it is not the building itself. It maintains a degree of abstraction that affords you the freedom to entertain and explore various options. You are not restricted to a particular process for a particular outcome. If you're interested in achieving translucency, for example, you can begin by investigating that quality through the selection of a material, a specific tool, a particular modeling technique, an applied technology, or any combination thereof.

Similarly, if you are composing a building's surface in a particular pattern, coupling that pattern with a material and making it three-dimensional leaves you with many important questions. How deep is the pattern? How is it distinguished from the field on which it appears? Is the pattern a reveal or is it part of a three-dimensional element? A conversation begins between the model and the concept, demanding that you deepen your original idea, that you fill it out.

Time has an impact as well, but it comes with more opportunities than constraints. While two-dimensional renderings and drawings force you to compile a totality out of discrete images, models allow a real-time view of your idea within one visual frame. The model helps you locate yourself in space. You are active in time around the object, and you can dissect it in time. Model making also lengthens time. While you are making something, you are in process mode, and your ideas have time to develop, moving between the brain, eye, and hand. Once you start building the model, other ideas will begin to flow, and you will find inspiration as you become comfortable translating design concepts into three dimensions.

This book will help the reader take the leap to fully integrate model making into your design process. The following pages present thirty-three concept blocks whose abstract nature and isolated conditions allow the reader to learn about various ways to investigate his or her own design ideas in three dimensions. The simple distilled form of each block isolates one or more modes of physical investigation, taking the complexity out of the making process and amplifying specific aspects or conditions of conceptual and representational design ideas. Each block is described in seven categories, including material, tools, tips and techniques, applied technologies and alternate methods, architectural concepts, a related existing model, and suggested alternatives. These categories are expanded in the corresponding appendices following the concept blocks. Here you will find supplemental information about materials, tools, and applied technologies, as well as a glossary of design concepts and additional tips and techniques.

Readers can peruse the book in whatever order they find most useful. They might want to flip through the concept blocks looking for inspiration, or read the appendices for information. Above all, I hope the book will encourage the reader to explore the many possibilities model making can bring to the art of design.

Acknowledgments

Model making is at its core a collaboration. Similarly, this book is a group effort, greatly enriched by the contributions of people within my community who I have worked with and learned from over the past three decades. The ideas presented in this book emanate from my life's involvement in architecture and design, starting with my education at Virginia Tech, which evolved into my business, zDp models, and my teaching position in design at California College of the Arts (CCA).

Thank you to the College of Architecture and Urban Studies at Virginia Tech and to my professors and mentors there: Lucie and Olivio Ferrari, Gene Egger, Hans Rott, and Ellen Braaten, who taught me to see the world through a making lens. I would also like to thank CCA for supporting the book with a faculty development grant and my students at CCA, who provide me with constant inspiration. I am also continually stimulated by the creative community in the building where my shop is located, the American Industrial Center, home to many creative minds.

I especially want to thank Clare Jacobson, formerly of Princeton Architectural Press, for so enthusiastically responding to an AIA lecture on craft and technology I gave in San Francisco in 2009 and approaching me to write this volume. Clare's immediate understanding of the concept and structure for the book was instrumental in getting it off the ground. Additionally, I would like to thank my editor, Nicola Bednarek Brower, for taking the book on and guiding it to its completion.

I am grateful to Emily Abruzzo for writing the preface, framing the emotional side of model making.

I would also like to recognize Dina Dobkin for assisting with the coordination and production of the manuscript. Dina also generated the instructional illustrations accompanying the Tips & Techniques. Brian Fong ably assisted in the production and postproduction of the photographs and illustrations. Thank you to Joanna Howser for jumping in toward the end to edit the text.

Thank you to the crew at zDp models, Eric Paulson, Ania Wagner, and Tudlik Moerk, for your invaluable help. Thanks also to Tim Culvahouse for translating my ideas into prose and Gerry Ratto, whom I have had the pleasure of working with for over a decade, for translating my ideas into images. I would like to acknowledge Kyle McDonald and Sarah Cohen for introducing graphic clarity to the initial book proposal.

I am grateful to Charlie Sheldon and Link Studios for allowing us to use their space for photography.

I would like to thank my parents, Tom and Jan Werner, and my sisters, Ann and Gail, for their support and love in all my creative endeavors.

Last but not least, I would like to thank my husband, Matthew Millman, not only for taking most of the beautiful photographs in this book but also for supporting me throughout the entire process.

Concept Blocks

Basswood Solid

Material
basswood solid

Tools
band saw / disc sander / sanding bed / template

Tips & Techniques

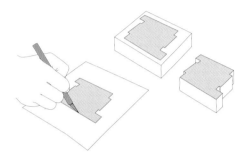

Create a complex solid by extruding the two-dimensional footprint of the desired form. Cut out a paper template from a print, plot, or hand drawing, and adhere it with double-stick tape or a spray adhesive to a block of solid material (wood, acrylic, foam, stacked composite). Roughly carve the shape with the band saw as described by the outline of the template, then sand it to achieve the accurate form. This is also a great way to make identical planes. Stack planes with double-stick tape and follow the instructions above. Then pry them apart with a thin metal ruler.

Applied Technologies & Alternate Methods
The basswood solid block was machined in a wood shop. Alternate methods for creating solids include 3-D printing (from a 3-D digital file), stereolithography, CNC milling, and laser-cutting. A CNC milling machine can cut a variety of solid materials and carve them into complex shapes, while with a laser you can cut multiple extruded solid shapes and stack them to create a solid mass.

Architectural Concepts
form / macro / opacity / scale / static / surface / volume

Sample Model (p. 142)

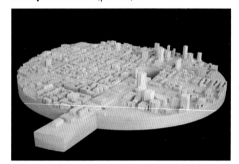

Suggested Alternatives

Bamboo solid   CNC-ed wood (p. 46)   Acrylic solid (p. 78)   Saw-cut solid (p. 82)   Stacked planes (p. 36)

*I would not have the model too exactly finished, not
too delicate and neat, but plain and simple—more to be
admired for the contrivance of the inventor than
the hand of the workman.*
LEON BATTISTA ALBERTI

Paint Surface

Materials
acrylic solid, acrylic urethane paint, primer

Tools
band saw / disc sander / foam tape / spray gun / stirring stick

Tips & Techniques

Handle an object for painting by adhering it with foam double-stick tape to an extension stick (such as a paint stirring stick). This allows you to spray all surfaces but one in one go without touching the object. Wait for the paint to dry and cure, then flip the object over to spray the final surface.

Applied Technologies & Alternate Methods
The painted surface block was created by first priming a sanded acrylic block and then spraying it with automotive-quality acrylic urethane paint (a clear coat tinted with opalescence). The addition of color can also be achieved with 3-D printing and laser-cutting, although 3-D printers provide only a limited color palette. Adhesive-backed color vinyl can be laser-cut and then adhered to a smooth-surfaced material for added detail and color. Alternatively, you can first adhere the color vinyl to the material and then laser-cut it.

Architectural Concepts
color / hue / opacity / materiality / monochrome / representation / surface

Sample Model (p. 142)

Suggested Alternatives

Stained wood

Sanded acrylic (p. 78)

Painted acrylic

Polished acrylic (p. 70)

Vinyl veneer

Architecture should speak of its time and place,
but yearn for timelessness.
FRANK GEHRY

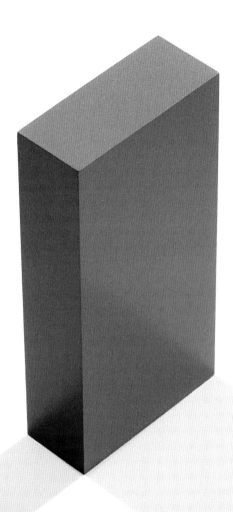

Gatorboard Core

Material
gatorboard

Tools
double-sided tape / metal ruler / sanding bed / X-Acto knife

Tips & Techniques

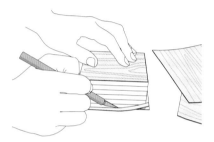

Create a gatorboard core by cutting identical footprint shapes of the desired extruded form, using a template and an X-Acto knife. Vertically stack the gatorboard layers, gluing them together one by one. The form of the stacked gatorboard can be further modified by cutting or sanding after it is assembled. Wood veneer or other thin materials can be adhered to a core form with numerous adhesives (depending on the materials used). A quick and effective adhesion method is double-sided tape. Make sure to cover the entire surface with adhesive to avoid buckling.

Applied Technologies & Alternate Methods
The gatorboard core block was made by hand. Solid core stacks for sheathing can also be created using a laser cutter or print/plot technology. A laser allows the designer to cut uniform complex layers of material, making registration for stacking precise. A template of the core shape can be printed from a digital file, adhered to a stack of material, and used as a cutting and sanding guide while machining.

Architectural Concepts
core / extrusion / massing / orientation / place / representation / surface

Sample Model (p. 142)

Suggested Alternatives

Acrylic core (p. 78)   Maple veneer   Foam substrate   Printed paper template (p. 42)   Cork veneer

Models are the only 3-D tool we know of, we have to remember that all so-called 3-D modeling done on the computer screen is two-dimensional.
EINAR JARMUND

Peeled Paper

Material
mat board with chipboard core

Tools
cutting mat / drafting equipment / metal ruler /
rice paper tape / tweezers / white glue / X-Acto knife

Tips & Techniques

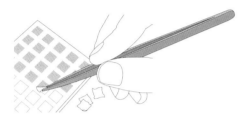

Create patterns on a facade by scoring a 2-ply mat
board and peeling off the outer thin paper layer
to reveal the inner chipboard core. You can draft the
patterns directly on the object by hand or adhere
a plot or print with low-tack adhesive to provide
a template. Use a metal ruler as a score guide for
your X-Acto knife.

Applied Technologies & Alternate Methods
The peeled paper block was made by hand out of
mat board and scored with an X-Acto knife. Surface
scoring can also be achieved with a laser or with the
help of print/plot technology. Use a laser to score
complex linework into a mat board that can then be
peeled by hand, or print linework and temporarily
adhere it onto the object to provide a template for
scoring.

Architectural Concepts
contrast / materiality / ornamentation /
representation / surface / texture

Sample Model (p. 143)

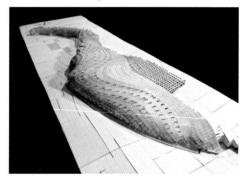

Suggested Alternatives

Laser-scored   Chipboard   Printed satellite   Task board   Printed rendering (p. 42)
basswood   topography

Architecture is a team effort, and model building promotes collaboration. A study model is easily modified by several designers during its development. Digital three-dimensional visualization is a powerful tool, but a solitary endeavor that limits design interaction and is not easily modified until it is substantially complete.
JERRY GRIFFIN

Basswood Screen

Material
basswood profiles

Tools
cutting mat / drafting equipment /
rice paper tape / sanding stick / styrene /
table saw / white glue / X-acto knife

Tips & Techniques

Create modulated complex structural elements by
using styrene and basswood profiles cut into uniform
lengths. Cutting the profiles slightly longer than
needed will allow you to sand them after assembly
to create an even line. Arrange the strips on a flat
surface, alternating basswood with styrene (with no
space in between), and hold them in place with a
weight (such as a metal square). Tape the assemblage
together and flip it over. Glue two or more basswood
elements perpendicular to the strips with white glue,
holding them down with a weight to mitigate warping.
Let dry before removing the tape and styrene spacers.
When making a styrene screen use basswood
spacers and solvent as the adhesive instead.

Applied Technologies & Alternate Methods
The basswood screen block was created by hand
using dimensional basswood and styrene spacers.
A screen can also be fabricated with a laser cutter,
by metal etching, or with print/plot technology.
Use a laser to cut screen patterns into various
materials, but note that there are material tolerance
limitations. You can etch a finer screen into metal and
add relief elements for more detail, or print graphic/
screen linework onto paper and adhere it to a form.

Architectural Concepts
grid / light / obstruction / pattern / rhythm / scale

Sample Model (p. 143)

Suggested Alternatives

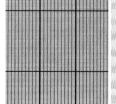

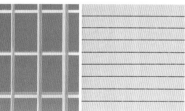

Metal etch linework

Alternating material
stack

Generic patterned
basswood

Saw-cut floor plates
(p. 66)

Saw-cut solid
(p. 82)

Simplicity is complexity resolved.
CONSTANTIN BRANCUSI

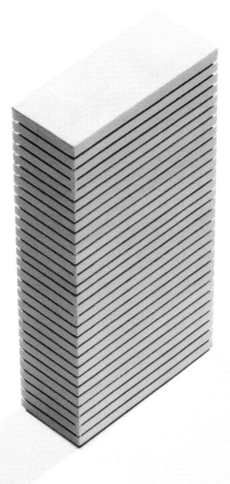

Composite Stack

Materials
acrylic sheet, basswood sheet

Tools
band saw / cutting mat / disc sander / double-stick tape / drafting tools / machinist block / metal ruler / sanding bed / sanding stick / template / X-Acto knife

Tips & Techniques

When creating a solid form from sheet materials, select a thickness that relates to the scale or architectural pattern of the project (floor-to-floor heights, slabs, window openings, grid, etc.). Stacking a series of different horizontal sections is also a quick way to create complex organic forms.

Applied Technologies & Alternate Methods
The composite stack block was created using machine tools and then assembled by hand. The individual components were cut on a band saw, stacked with double-stick tape, and then sanded into shape using a printed template of the footprint. Composite solids can also be sculpted with a CNC mill, which can carve composite material stock into complex forms, or a laser, which is able to cut composite layers into the desired form.

Architectural Concepts
additive / contrast / extrusion / hybrid / layer / light / line / progression / scale / solid/void / stack / translucency

Sample Model (p. 143)

Suggested Alternatives

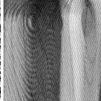
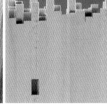

Stacked cardboard

CNC-ed solid (p. 46)

Composite of profiles (p. 74)

Basswood screen (p. 26)

Stacked gatorboard (p. 22)

Architecture is the masterly, correct, and magnificent play of masses brought together in light.
LE CORBUSIER

Styrene Relief

Materials
patterned styrene sheets

Tools
acrylic solvent / cutting mat / drafting equipment,
machinist block / metal ruler / rice paper tape /
sanding stick / X-Acto knife

Tips & Techniques

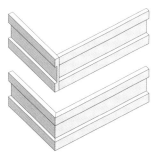

Create a beveled edge joint by hand-sanding the
styrene sheets on a 45-degree jig or routing them on
a machine. A butt joint will not allow the relief pattern
to continue seamlessly around the corner, while a
beveled joint enables the pattern to turn the corner
without interruption.

Applied Technologies & Alternate Methods
The styrene relief block was constructed by hand
using patterned styrene sheets. Styrene can also be
used in conjunction with a CNC mill, a laser cutter,
and metal etching. Use a CNC mill to create a mold
for vacuforming polystyrene, or a laser to cut and
score styrene sheets. Dimensional styrene can also
be applied to a metal-etched or laser-cut grid guide to
create a screen.

Architectural Concepts
texture / scale / revolve / rhythm / relief / surface /
representation

Sample Model (p. 144)

Suggested Alternatives

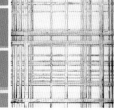

Generic patterned
basswood

Vacuformed styrene
(p. 62)

Styrene elements
(p. 80)

Styrene structure
(p. 66)

Saw-cut relief
(p. 44)

Art does not reproduce what we see;
rather it makes us see.
PAUL KLEE

Flocked Surface

Materials

ground foam, cardstock

Tools

brush / cutting mat / double-sided tape / metal ruler / sieve / white glue diluted with water / X-Acto knife

Tips & Techniques

Adhere double-sided tape as a continuous surface to the back of green cardstock. To ensure it will stay flat, tape the perimeter to a piece of wood or a tabletop surface with the (unpeeled) double-stick side facing down. Brush a thin glaze of diluted white glue (approximately 1:1 dilution with water) onto the top of the cardstock. Sift the ground foam through a sieve until the surface of the cardstock is no longer showing visible glue or dampness. The drying time varies, but twenty-four hours is recommended. Gently vacuum or brush off extra ground foam once the glue has dried. If the flock is spotty, repeat the process.

Applied Technologies & Alternate Methods

The flocked block was made by hand, using ground foam and a matching color cardstock. Ground foam can also be applied to materials that are CNC-ed or laser-cut. You can flock a complex CNC-ed surface in the same way as a flat sheet. If landscape pads are irregular, flock sheets of material and then laser-cut them into the desired shapes.

Architectural Concepts

abstraction / haptic / landscape / organic / site / surface / texture

Sample Model (p. 144)

Suggested Alternatives

Flocked metal tree

Printed satellite topography

CNC-ed foam topography (p. 34)

Green cork

Stained wood

*The aim of art is to represent not the outward
appearance of things, but their inward significance.*
ARISTOTLE

Foam Topography

Material
polyurethane foam

Tools
digital file of topography plotted to model scale / pantograph

Tips & Techniques

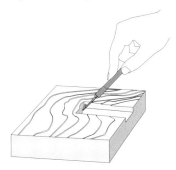

Sculpt the foam topography with hand tools such as chisel blades, small metal spatulas, X-Acto knives, or scrapers to inlay roads, buildings, and landscape elements. If you have removed too much foam, make a filler patch with ground foam and white glue.

Applied Technologies & Alternate Methods
The foam topography block was made with a router (pantograph), using a scaled plot as template. You can also use a CNC mill or a laser to create complex topography. A CNC milling machine generates topography from a 3-D digital file. Individual layers can also be laser-cut and stacked.

Architectural Concepts
erosion / grade / gradient / landscape / mapping / organic / relief / scale / site / topography

Sample Model (p. 145)

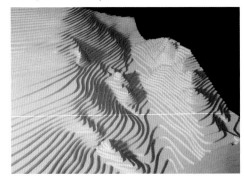

Suggested Alternatives

Flocked surface
(p. 32)

Chipboard
topography

CNC-ed topography
(p. 46)

Polyurethane
foam

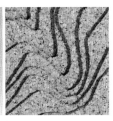
Cork topography
(p. 76)

*Great architecture offers shapes and surfaces
molded for the pleasurable touch of the eye.*
JUHANI PALLASMAA

Smooth Topography

Material
basswood sheets

Tools
band saw / brush / contact cement / cutting mat /
disc sander / Dremel / grinder / metal ruler /
palm sander / sandpaper / sanding stick / template /
white glue / X-Acto knife

Tips & Techniques

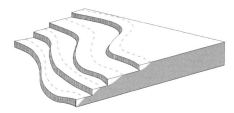

Create a smooth and semiaccurate grade in a
topographic model through cutting and sanding.
Modify the scaled topographic drawing by offsetting
the topographic lines to create cut lines that reflect
the excess material needed to sand back to the
original contour lines. Lightly trace the original lines
on the cut topographic planes, stack the layers, and
palm-sand them back to the original lines.

Applied Technologies & Alternate Methods
The smooth topography block was created by
stacking basswood planes and sanding the surface
smooth. Complex, smooth, organic forms can also
be created through 3-D printing/stereolithography,
CNC milling, or laser-cutting. A 3-D printer prints the
topographic form using additive layering technology,
while a CNC mill carves a topographic surface by
subtraction from a solid slab of material. You can also
use a laser to cut individual topography layers, which
can then be stacked into a solid and sanded smooth.

Architectural Concepts
contours / layers / massing / plane / relief / site /
topography / undulate

Sample Model (p. 145)

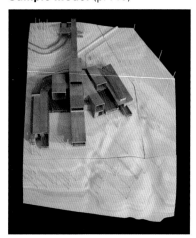

Suggested Alternatives

Stacked composite
(p. 28)

CNC-ed solid
(p. 46)

**Composite of
profiles** (p. 74)

**Subtractive
topography** (p. 34)

**Additive
topography**

*Architects are taught to privilege the visual
and be seduced by images. But we live in all five
of our senses.*
HILLARY BROWN

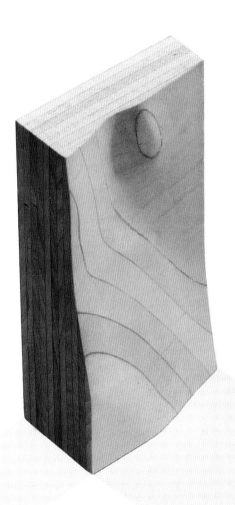

Cement Pour

Materials
cement / water

Tools
bucket / mold / mold release / stirring stick

Tips & Techniques

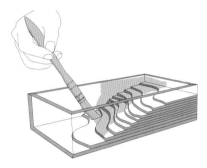

Create a continuous barrier seal on the mold. Its surface should be smooth and free of crevices, undercuts, and irregularities that might interfere with the separation of the object from the mold. Depending on the material used to create the mold, a release should be applied to the surfaces. Releases for molds range from specific sprays to household agents such as oil soap, Vaseline, and cooking oil spray.

Applied Technologies & Alternate Methods
The cement pour block was created using a machine-made mold and cement mix. A mold can be fabricated with 3-D printing/stereolithography or CNC milling. You can also cut planes on a laser and assemble them into a mold.

Architectural Concepts
density / form / inversion / mass / positive / relief / slab / solid

Sample Model (p. 145)

Suggested Alternatives

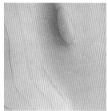

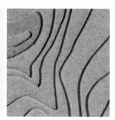

Organic solid from planes (p. 36)

Stereolithographic organic interior space

Bent acrylic

Plaster pour (p. 40)

Chipboard mold

Technical skill is mastery of complexity, while creativity is mastery of simplicity.
CHRISTOPHER ZEEMAN

Plaster Pour

Materials
plaster, water

Tools
bucket / mold / mold release / stirring stick

Tips & Techniques

Slowly sift the appropriate amount of plaster powder into a bucket of water by hand, until an island of plaster has formed. Mix water and plaster by hand or with a drill mixer until it is smooth and consistent, before pouring it into the mold.

Applied Technologies & Alternate Methods
The plaster pour block was made using a machine-made mold and plaster mix. A mold can be fabricated with 3-D printing/stereolithography or CNC milling. You can also cut planes on a laser and assemble them into a mold.

Architectural Concepts
form / mass / materiality / negative / opaque / organic / relief / sculpture / smooth / translate

Sample Model (p. 146)

Suggested Alternatives

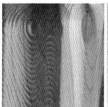
CNC-ed mold (p. 46)

Sculpted foam

Resin pour

Vacuformed mold (p. 62)

3-D printed complex form (p. 52)

Since architecture is a visual physical experience of space made of real materials, we find physical models to be the best way to study the sensory experience we're trying to achieve. Working with physical models engages the optics of the human eye such as the cone of vision and depth of field that cannot be replicated on a screen.
MARTIN COX, BADE STAGEBERG COX

Paper Print

Materials
mat board, plotted elevations at model scale (a black-and-white copy for the template plus a fully rendered presentation drawing)

Tools
cutting mat / double-sided tape / metal ruler / printer / scale / spray adhesive / X-Acto knife

Tips & Techniques

Adhere black-and-white templates of elevations and plans to mat board with a low-tack spray adhesive. Cut out the scale elevations and assemble them into a three-dimensional form. Peel off the black-and-white template prints and replace them with rendered color elevations for the final presentation.

Applied Technologies & Alternate Methods
The paper print block was made by hand out of mat board with a printed bond paper veneer. Methods of applying digital information to planar material include laser-cutting and printing/plotting. You can use a laser to score linework onto a facade or a printer/plotter to print graphic information on various materials, including wood veneer, cardstock, and colored papers.

Architectural Concepts
diagram / elevation / envelope / facade / graphic / realism / representation / scale

Sample Model (p. 146)

Suggested Alternatives

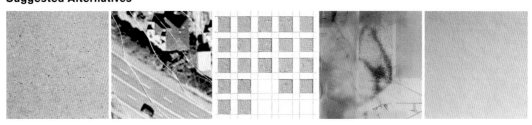

Chipboard   Printed satellite   Scored paper (p. 24)   Printed acetate (p. 56)   Mat board
                 topography

*The divine is immaterial; it has no definite, specific
forms; it is invisible. The work of art, on the other hand,
is by necessity material; it has definite, specific forms;
and it is completely rooted in the realm of the visible
and tangible, in the field of sensuous experience.*
MOSHE BARASCH

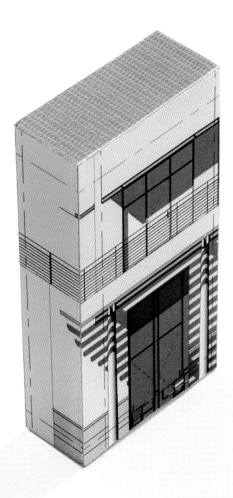

Acrylic Reveal

Materials
acrylic solid, graphite dust

Tools
band saw / drafting equipment / machinist square /
sanding stick / table saw

Tips & Techniques

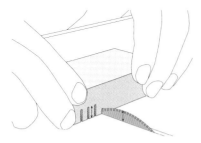

Create a reveal in a solid material with the table saw
by adjusting the height of the saw blade to match
the depth of the desired reveal. Consider the blade
thickness when notching, as this will determine the
width of the reveal. Rotate the object to cut
a continuous reveal.

Applied Technologies & Alternate Methods
The acrylic reveal block was fabricated by notching
a pattern into an acrylic solid with a table saw. You
can also create relief elements with 3-D printing/
stereolithography, CNC milling, laser-cutting, or metal
etching. A 3-D printer can print forms with an organic
surface relief from a digital file. You can also carve
surface texture into a solid with a CNC mill, or laser-
cut relief elements out of planar material and adhere
them to a solid. The half-etch technique can produce
relief elements in metal-etch parts.

Architectural Concepts
contrast / figure/ground / grid / hatched / line /
matrix / pattern / relief / reveal / rhythm / solid/void /
texture, translucency

Sample Model (p. 146)

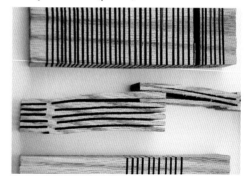

Suggested Alternatives

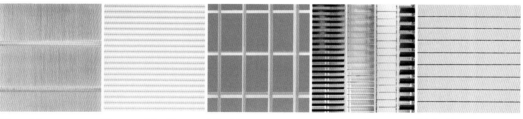

Inlay notch   Styrene relief pattern   3-D grid   Metal-etch relief   Notched basswood
                     (p. 30)   (p. 66)   (p. 50)   (p. 82)

Design in art is a recognition of the relation between various things, various elements in the creative flux. You can't invent a design. You recognize it, in the fourth dimension. That is, with your blood and your bones, as well as with your eyes.
D. H. LAWRENCE

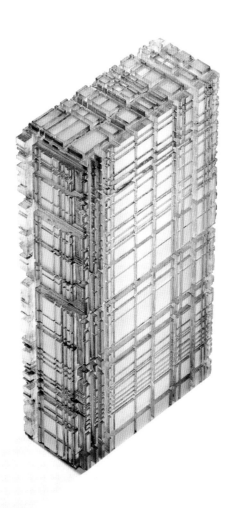

CNC Topography

Materials
plywood, wood

Tools
3-D digital files / CNC mill / sandpaper

Tips & Techniques

Cut negative and positive forms separately to seamlessly join when assembled.

Applied Technologies & Alternate Methods
The CNC topography block was fabricated of plywood using CNC milling technology. Complex organic shapes can also be 3-D printed. 3-D printing/ stereolithography is especially useful for modeling complex internal spaces.

Architectural Concepts
continuous / fluidity / form / juxtaposition / relief, sculptural / site / subtraction / surface / topography

Sample Model (p. 147)

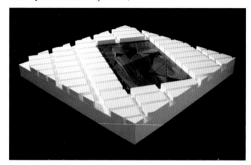

Suggested Alternatives

Chipboard topography

CNC form as vacuform mold (p. 62)

Stereolithographic organic interior space

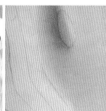
Sanded organic topography (p. 36)

CNC-ed foam (p. 34)

An attempt at visualizing the Fourth Dimension:
Take a point, stretch it into a line, curl it into a circle,
twist it into a sphere, and punch through the sphere.
ALBERT EINSTEIN

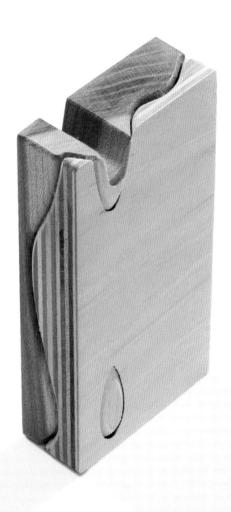

Stereolithography

Material
photopolymer

Tools
stereolithography file / 3-D software / stereolithography machine

Tips & Techniques

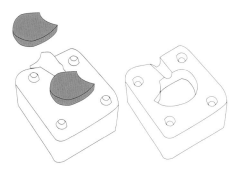

Objects created through stereolithography can be used as molds to translate precise forms into other materials such as resin, plaster, or porcelain. For example, you can use a photopolymer print to create a plaster mold for slip casting multiple identical porcelain objects.

Applied Technologies & Alternate Methods
The stereolithography block was created by first drawing the form using 3-D software and then printing it on a stereolithography machine. Complex forms can also be CNC-ed or laser-cut. The CNC mill carves complex surface relief patterns, while a laser can cut planar layers for assemblage into a three-dimensional form.

Architectural Concepts
additive / appearance / flexibility / form / layering / organic / radial / rotation / scale / translation

Sample Model (p. 147)

Suggested Alternatives

3-D printed complex form (p. 52)

Vacuform mold stereolithography (p. 62)

Plaster mold stereolithography (p. 40)

Resin

Bent acrylic

Architectural models are based on a sapience of materialization by which materiality becomes the carrier of fluid and invisible thoughts.
MARCO FRASCARI

Metal Etch Screen

Material
stainless-steel plate

Tools
chisel blade / superglue / tweezers / vector file /
X-Acto knife

Tips & Techniques

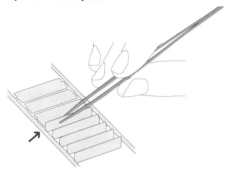

Create a three-dimensional louver relief by etching a
louver pattern into a stainless-steel plate. Leave small
connector tabs to the left and right of the louvers
and then twist the louver elements into position with
tweezers. Half-etching the metal along the fold lines
allows for easy and precise folding.

Applied Technologies & Alternate Methods
The metal etch screen block was generated by
etching a stainless-steel plate with acid and modifying
the etched parts. You can also create surface texture
with a CNC mill or laser. A CNC mill can carve into
a solid to create texture, but there are size and scale
limitations. Use a laser to cut and score linework onto
model parts.

Architectural Concepts
detail / enclosure / hierarchy / interface /
ornamentation / pattern / scale / screening / surface

Sample Model (p. 148)

Suggested Alternatives

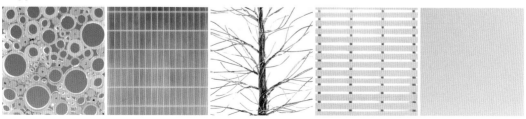

Styrene relief elements
(p. 80)

Laser-scored linework
(p. 60)

Metal wire tree
profile

Basswood screen
(p. 26)

Metallic paint for
representation (p. 20)

Values become engulfed in miniature,
and miniature causes men to dream.
GASTON BACHELARD

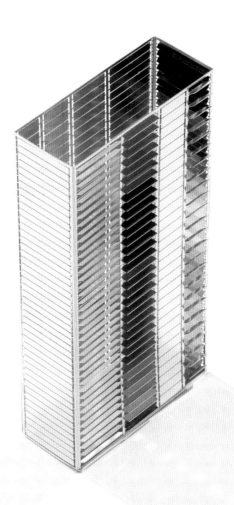

3-D Print

Materials
resin, CA (cyanoacrylate) binder (superglue)

Tools
3-D file / 3-D modeling software / 3-D printer

Tips & Techniques

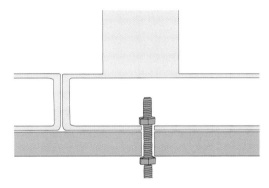

3-D print materials have surface integrity only, as merely a thin layer is cured to a solid, while the core of the print remains in powder form. If you are planning to attach objects to a 3-D print or to attach the print itself to another object, design a hole into the 3-D print. This hole will have more structural integrity than if you drill into the print, because of the powder interior.

Applied Technologies & Alternate Methods
The 3-D-printed block was fabricated using 3-D printing technology; after a digital 3-D file is created, it is printed additively layer by layer. You can also generate complex organic shapes using a CNC mill, a laser cutter, or stereolithography. The CNC carves a relief subtractively into a solid form, while stereolithography prints complex forms that can later be machined and surface-finished. Using a laser, you can cut planar layers and assemble them by hand into a three-dimensional form.

Architectural Concepts
additive / asymmetry / diagonal / disintegration / folding / mass / monochromatic / obstruction / solid/void

Sample Model (p. 148)

Suggested Alternatives

Poured complex form (p. 38)

Complex form stereolithography (p. 48)

Vacuformed complex surface (p. 62)

CNC-ed wood (p. 46)

CNC-ed foam (p. 34)

I don't think of form as a kind of architecture.
The architecture is the result of the forming.
It is the kinesthetic and visual sense of position and
wholeness that puts the thing into the realm of art.
ROY LICHTENSTEIN

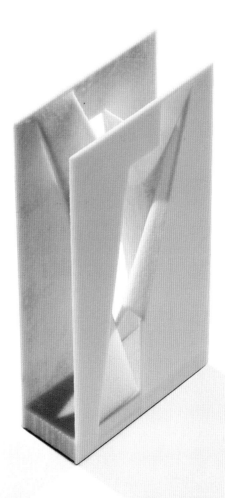

Interior Surface Spray

Materials
acrylic sheet, acrylic urethane paint

Tools
acrylic solvent / miter machine / table saw

Tips & Techniques

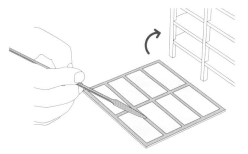

Spray-painting an interior surface is an easy method to conceal glue marks when working with acrylic. Spray the pattern of the glue joint onto the acrylic in a color similar to the color of the structure you wish to adhere. Apply glue to the sprayed surface pattern and adhere the structure to the acrylic.

Applied Technologies & Alternate Methods
The interior surface spray block was made using spray-painted acrylic sheets. You can also create a polished colored surface by adhering a thin film of vinyl to the interior surface of a clear acrylic sheet. This vinyl-backed acrylic sheet can then be laser-cut and assembled with the vinyl side facing in.

Architectural Concepts
color / depth / glazing / opacity / plane / reflective / surface

Sample Model (p. 149)

Suggested Alternatives

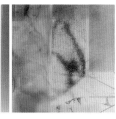

Vinyl veneer

Color acrylic (p. 58)

Polished acrylic (p. 70)

Acrylic with acetate overlay (p. 56)

Painted acrylic (p. 20)

*The task of the architectural project is to reveal,
through transformation of form, the essence of the
surrounding context.*
VITTORIO GREGOTTI

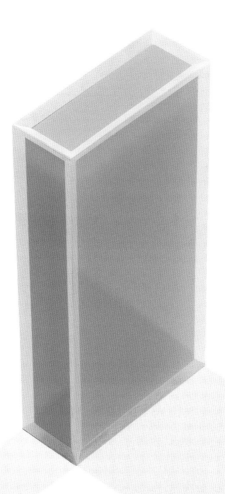

Acetate

Materials
acetate sheet, acrylic sheet

Tools
cutting mat / metal ruler / printer / scissors / spray adhesive / X-Acto knife

Tips & Techniques

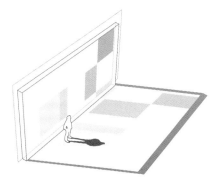

Overlay colored acetate sheets with planar acrylic to add color, scale, and linework to transparent glazing.

Applied Technologies & Alternate Methods
The acetate block was made by hand by adhering printed acetate film to an acrylic sheet. Graphic information and color can be added to a model using a laser cutter, metal etch technique, or through printing/plotting technology. Use a laser to score graphic information onto acrylic, which can then be masked and sprayed with paint, or rub color into linework half-etched into metal or laser-scored into acrylic. Color information can also be printed onto paper and adhered to a surface.

Architectural Concepts
animation / color / interaction / film / layering / materiality / narrative / projection / scale / space / translucency / transparency

Sample Model (p. 149)

Suggested Alternatives

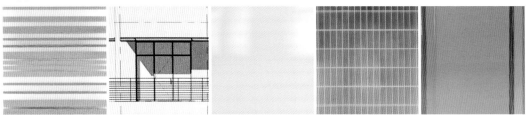

Acrylic as glazing
(p. 28)

Printed paper rendering
(p. 42)

Interior surface spray
(p. 54)

Laser-scored glazing
(p. 60)

Color acrylic
(p. 58)

*There's nothing worse than a brilliant image
of a fuzzy concept.*
ANSEL ADAMS

Color Acrylic

Material
color acrylic sheet

Tools
acrylic solvent / band saw / disc sander / rice paper tape / sanding stick / scoring tool / table saw

Tips & Techniques

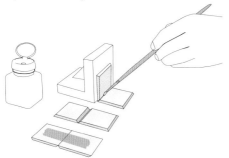

Polishing and temporarily hinging the beveled edges of the acrylic together with tape will help you achieve a cleaner joint. Polished edges can be achieved through wet/dry sanding or flaming the edges with heat. When working with polished edges, use acrylic solvent adhesive, applied with an animal-hair brush.

Applied Technologies & Alternate Methods
The color acrylic block was assembled by hand, using manufactured color acrylic sheets. Translucent color can be added to a model with the help of a laser cutter or printing/plotting technology. Laser-cut and -score acrylic, then mask and paint it. A similar translucent color effect can be achieved by backing acrylic with printed acetate film.

Architectural Concepts
color / enclosure / envelope / hue / light / opacity / plane / reflective / saturation / space / surface / transparency

Sample Model (p. 150)

Suggested Alternatives

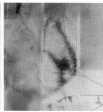

Interior surface spray (p. 54)

Polished acrylic (p. 70)

Sanded acrylic (p. 78)

Acrylic with printed acetate overlay (p. 56)

Painted acrylic (p. 20)

Color is sensibility in material form,
matter in its primordial state.
YVES KLEIN

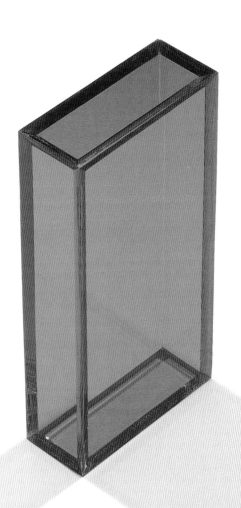

Laser-Score

Material
acrylic sheet, acrylic solid

Tools
acrylic solvent / band saw / brush / disc sander / laser cutter / rice paper tape / sanding stick / table saw / vector drawing optimized for laser

Tips & Techniques

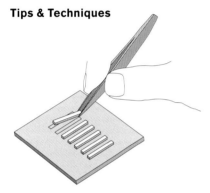

Represent detailed linework with laser scores, or use them as an assembly guide for relief elements. Styrene profile elements can be readily cut and adhered to laser-scored linework to express exterior elements, structure, and sunshades.

Applied Technologies & Alternate Methods
The laser-score block was assembled using laser-cut and -scored acrylic sheets, sheathed over a machined solid translucent acrylic core. Score lines can also be created with 3-D printing/stereolithography, metal etching, and print/plot technology. Using a 3-D printer, you can print linework as a score pattern. Half-etching produces score lines in the metal etch process. You can also print linework on paper and adhere it to an object or draw directly on the model.

Architectural Concepts
envelope / grid / line / pattern / reflective / rhythm / translucency / transparency

Sample Model (p. 150)

Suggested Alternatives

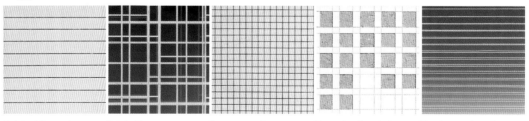

Notched linework (p. 82)   Painted laser scores (p. 64)   Laser-scored basswood   Scored and peeled paper (p. 24)   Hand-scored acrylic (p. 68)

A great building must begin with the unmeasurable,
must go through measurable means when it is being
designed, and in the end must be unmeasurable.
LOUIS KAHN

Vacuform

Material
polystyrene

Tools
mold / vacuform machine

Tips & Techniques

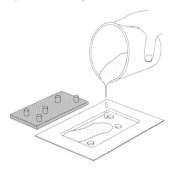

Vacuformed polystyrene shells are ready to use as molds. Rarely does an undercut exist in a vacuformed mold, increasing the chance of a successful release of the object from the mold.

Applied Technologies & Alternate Methods
The vacuform block was fabricated by vacuforming polystyrene over a machined wood solid form. Stryene can also be formed over molds made with a CNC mill, a laser, or stereolithography. Molds for the vacuformer can be made of many materials, such as foam, wood, acrylic, or metal. The method of fabrication depends on the appropriate selection of material and the complexity of the form.

Architectural Concepts
diagonal / oblique / surface / envelope / organic / shell / fluidity / translucency / tent

Sample Model (p. 151)

Suggested Alternatives

Stereolithographic organic interior space

Vacuformed mold for plaster pour (p. 38)

Heat-bent acrylic

CNC-ed mold for vacuforming (p. 46)

Styrene relief (p. 30)

Don't fight forces, use them.
BUCKMINSTER FULLER

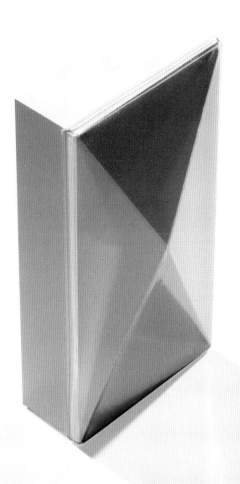

Paint Mask

Materials
laser-cut and -scored acrylic sheet with manufacturer's protective masking

Tools
band saw / brush / CAD drawings / disc sander / paint / primer / rice paper tape / sanding stick / scale / scoring tool / table saw / tweezers

Tips & Techniques

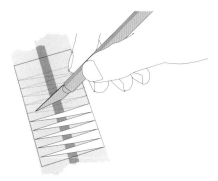

Prepare a laser-scored acrylic part for painting by using the laser scores as cut guides for a mask of rice paper tape. The X-Acto knife blade easily slips into the score groove, guiding the blade along the score for a perfect mask outline of the desired pattern to be painted.

Applied Technologies & Alternate Methods
The paint mask block was assembled by hand, using laser-cut and double-scored acrylic sheets; after cutting and scoring, the manufacturer's protective mask was peeled off in the areas between the scores to apply paint. You can create guides for masking and painting with a laser or through metal etching. Rub latex paint into a laser-scored line or a half-etched score on metal to add color to linework, or use scores as a masking guide prior to painting.

Architectural Concepts
glaze / grid / line / pattern / sequence / structure

Sample Model (p. 151)

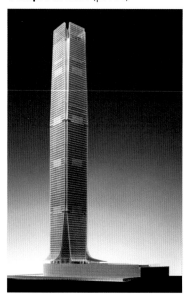

Suggested Alternatives

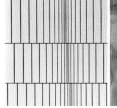

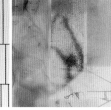

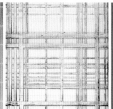

| Metal-etched linework | Acrylic with printed acetate overlay (p. 56) | Laser-scored acrylic (p. 60) | Saw-cut acrylic (p. 44) | Painted acrylic |

Think with the senses, feel with the mind.
ROBERT STORR

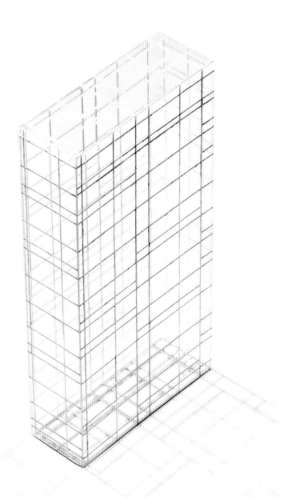

Stacked Plates

Materials
acrylic sheet, styrene profiles

Tools
brush / disc sander / drafting tools / gatorboard jig / sanding stick / scale drawing of building section / table saw

Tips & Techniques

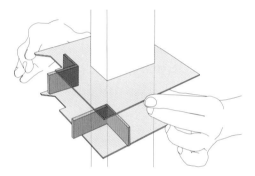

Stack acrylic plates using spacer jigs equivalent in size to the floor-to-floor dimension of your model minus the thickness of material used for the floor plate. The spacer jigs can be made out of gatorboard and are more stable if they have an L-shape. Thread styrene rods through the plate holes and glue the plates to the rods before removing the spacer jigs.

Applied Technologies & Alternate Methods
The stacked plates block was assembled by hand using machined acrylic plates and styrene rods. Alternate methods for creating an open stack include 3-D printing/stereolithography and laser-cutting. A 3-D printer can print a stack as a single form, while you can use a laser to cut acrylic plates with column and core holes for threading and stacking. Alternatively, you can use a drill press to bore column holes through a stack of plates.

Architectural Concepts
circulation / framing / intersection / penetration / platform / slab / span / structure / verticality

Sample Model (p. 152)

Suggested Alternatives

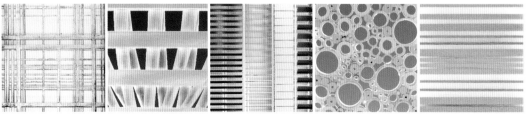

Saw-cut reveals
(p. 44)

Floor-plate stack
stereolithography (p. 48)

Metal etch with tabs
(p. 50)

Styrene elements
(p. 80)

Alternating material
stack (p. 28)

*In architecture the line and the two-dimensional area
do not exist—they are mathematical abstractions.
Architecture is always three-dimensional—even in
a micro-thin layer of paint.*
ANDREA DEPLAZES

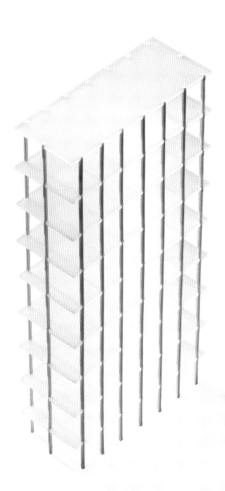

Hand-Scored

Material
acrylic solid

Tools
drafting tools / metal ruler / rice paper tape / scoring tool

Tips & Techniques

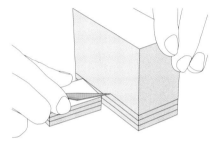

Creating your own hand-scoring tool will help you achieve even score lines. Cut a number of acrylic squares in a thickness that matches the desired dimension between scores. The quantity of cut squares should be equal to the height of the entire score pattern when stacked (or half the height if the object you are scoring can be flipped). Adhere an X-Acto blade to one of the acrylic squares. On an even surface, slide the acrylic square with the dull side of the blade along the vertical surface of the object to create a score. Add an acrylic square to the bottom of the stack and repeat until your score pattern is complete. This is a great technique for applying scores to curvilinear model parts.

Applied Technologies & Alternate Methods
The hand-scored block was created by scoring a polished acrylic solid at equal intervals using the back side of an X-Acto blade. Material can also be scored with a CNC mill, a laser cutter, or the metal etch process. You can rout a reveal line on a CNC mill or score linework into a variety of materials with a laser cutter. When working with metal, you can half-etch it to create a score line. Each method has tolerances dictated by your choice of material.

Architectural Concepts
grid / incremental / joint / line / pattern / scale / texture

Sample Model (p. 152)

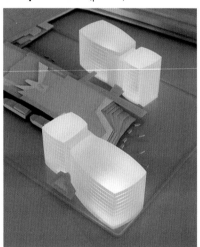

Suggested Alternatives

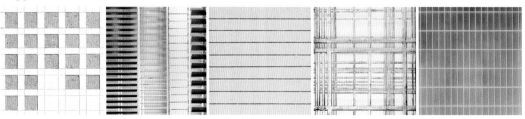

Scored and peeled paper (p. 24)

Metal-etched scores (p. 50)

Saw-cut linework (p. 82)

Saw-cut reveals (p. 44)

Laser-scored acrylic (p. 60)

The common eye sees only the outside of things, and judges by that, but the seeing eye pierces through and reads the heart and the soul, finding there capacities which the outside didn't indicate or promise, and which the other kind of eye couldn't detect.
MARK TWAIN

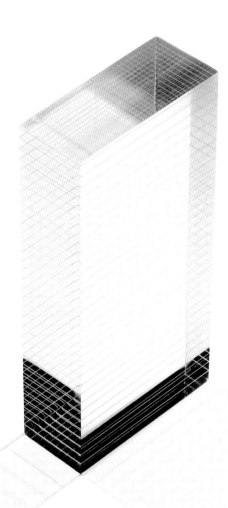

Polished Acrylic

Material
acrylic solid

Tools
band saw / clean cotton cloth / disc sander / polishing cream / sandpaper / sanding stick / table saw / dry sandpaper / wet/dry sandpaper

Tips & Techniques

Cut or sculpt acrylic into the desired form. Sand it with dry sandpaper (150–220 grit) and wet/dry sandpaper (220–800 grit) until scratches become cloudy or frostlike in appearance. Polish the object with heavy scratch remover cream, followed by fine scratch remover cream, then clean it with antistatic cleaner and a clean cotton cloth.

Applied Technologies & Alternate Methods
The polished acrylic block was fabricated in the machine shop and polished by hand. A polished surface can also be created with a laser or stereo-lithography. Laser-cutting creates a polished cut edge on an acrylic sheet, while photopolymer used for stereolithography can be rubbed with vegetable oil to create a shiny surface. You can also apply a clear coat to a sanded surface to achieve a polished finish.

Architectural Concepts
form / glazing / light / reflectivity / space / surface / translucency / transparency

Sample Model (p. 153)

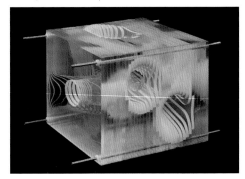

Suggested Alternatives

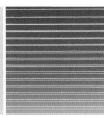
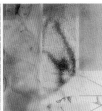

Color acrylic (p. 58)

Vacuformed styrene surface (p. 62)

Hand-scored acrylic (p. 68)

Acrylic with printed acetate overlay (p. 56)

Sanded acrylic (p. 78)

It's not what you look at that matters, it's what you see.
HENRY DAVID THOREAU

Bent Acrylic

Material
acrylic sheet

Tools
band saw / disc sander / heat gun / sandpaper / spindle sander / table saw / template / wood mold

Tips & Techniques

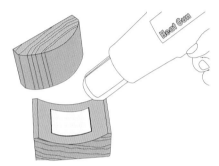

Create organic shapes with planar acrylic through heat bending. Make a template of the desired curve and cut and sand negative and positive wood molds. Offset the molds by the thickness of the acrylic material. Span the flat acrylic sheet across the negative curved wood mold and apply heat with a heat gun in an even fashion. Place (do not press) the positive curve mold on top of the acrylic once it has dropped or bent into the negative curve position. Allow the wood mold to pull the heat out of the acrylic part. Remove the negative mold and let the acrylic rest on the positive mold. Be prepared to make multiple parts and select the best.

Applied Technologies & Alternate Methods
The bent acrylic block was fabricated by hand using machine-cut acrylic sheets and a machined wood mold. Alternative methods for creating organic forms include 3-D printing/stereolithography, laser-cutting, and bending etched metal. Complex organic forms can be printed with a 3-D printer, or you can unwrap them in CAD, laser-cut them, and then bend them into appropriate shapes. Etched metal can be bent around a curvilinear mold form.

Architectural Concepts
concave / convex / envelope / flexibility / fluid / negative / organic / scale / surface / symmetry / tangential

Sample Model (p. 153)

Suggested Alternatives

Bent wood

Bendable task board

Plaster-poured organic form (p. 40)

Bent styrene (p. 62)

Bendable veneer

To experiment is at first more valuable than to produce;
free play in the beginning develops courage.
JOSEF ALBERS

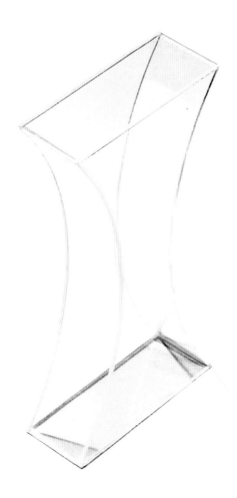

Basswood Profiles

Material
basswood profiles

Tools
disc sander / drafting equipment / sanding stick / table saw / white glue

Tips & Techniques

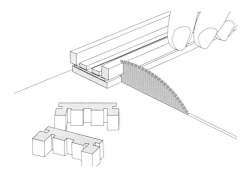

Bond simple profile elements together to create a complex extrusion profile of a desired footprint. Slice the profile into multiple uniform parts as needed, using a small-blade table saw.

Applied Technologies & Alternate Methods
The basswood profiles block was created by bonding together dimensional basswood elements and sanding them into shape. Alternate fabrication methods include CNC milling and laser-cutting. The CNC mill can sculpt composite material stock, while you can custom-cut profile elements with a laser and combine them.

Architectural Concepts
animation / convergence / dimension / disintegration / joint / lamination / micro / ornamentation / pattern / rhythm / structure / surface

Sample Model (p. 153)

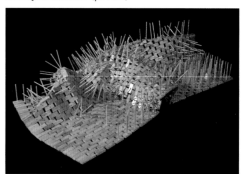

Suggested Alternatives

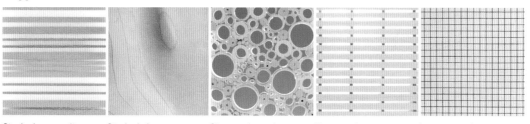

Stacked composite
(p. 28)

Stacked planes
(p. 36)

Styrene elements
(p. 80)

Basswood screen
(p. 26)

Laser-scored
basswood

*While they instigate a relationship between an actual
observer with a physical artifact, physical models
make possible a disembodied yet holistic approach;
by locating the eye at a distance from a scaled-down
representation of the project, physical models allow the
evaluation of abstract concepts (massing, composition,
proportion) that govern the relationship between the
parts to the whole.*
JOEL SANDERS

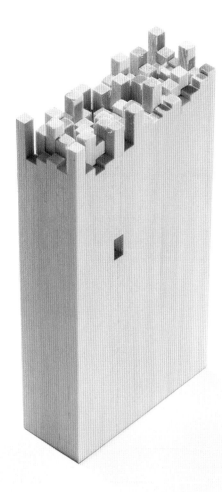

Cork Topography

Material
basswood profiles

Tools
adhesive / plotted grading plan / X-Acto knife

Tips & Techniques

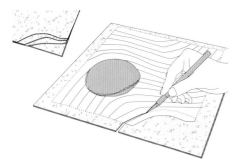

Transfer topographic information by placing a plotted grading plan directly onto a sheet of cork. Weigh down the drawing with beanbags so it does not move. Starting with the lowest grade, cut directly through the paper and cork, following the line to the edge of the base border to allow for a more precise registration during assembly. Move the grading plan onto an uncut cork sheet to cut out the next topographic layer, and repeat until all topographic layers have been cut out. Stack the topographic layers and glue them together in sets of two, then sets of four layers, etc., to assure precise registration.

Applied Technologies & Alternate Methods
The cork topography block was fabricated by hand using cork sheeting, cut to shape with an X-Acto knife. Alternate methods for creating cork topography include CNC milling and laser-cutting. The CNC mill can carve into a stacked cork form to create a topographic surface. You can also cut individual cork planes with a laser and then assemble them by hand.

Architectural Concepts
ascension / contours / grade / gradient / ground / mapping / organic / overlapping / plane / layer / scale / site / texture

Sample Model (p. 154)

Suggested Alternatives

Green cork

Flocked surface (p. 32)

CNC-ed foam topography (p. 34)

Printed satellite topography

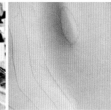

Basswood topography (p. 36)

A model cannot trigger all possible stories about the modeled object so a model is in some way specialized and limited. Of course, if all these accounts of the model and the object being modeled were the same then the objects would be indistinguishable and we might even conclude that they were the same object.
JOHN MONK

Sanded Acrylic

Material
acrylic solid

Tools
drafting tools / sanding bed / sandpaper / table saw

Tips & Techniques

Sanding acrylic creates a translucent surface that can add depth and aid in light transmission. Use a sanded acrylic core threaded through the model and base to transmit light from below the base, illuminating the model. Light leaks can be addressed with black tape or by spraying surfaces black or silver surrounding the core and under the base.

Applied Technologies & Alternate Methods
The sanded acrylic block was fabricated in the machine shop out of a one-inch-thick sheet of acrylic, cut to size, and then sanded by hand on a sanding bed. To achieve a sanded texture you can also laser-score the acrylic with very tight successive linework. Spraying acrylic with Dulcote is another alternative.

Architectural Concepts
edge / form / geometric / light / materiality / surface / translucency / visibility

Sample Model (p. 154)

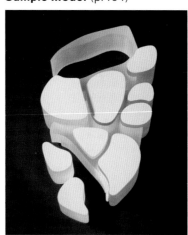

Suggested Alternatives

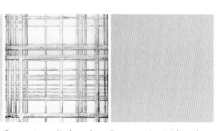

Translucent resin pour   Polished acrylic (p. 70)   Painted acrylic (p. 20)   Saw-cut acrylic (p. 44)   Basswood solid (p. 18)

*A designer knows that he has achieved perfection
not when there is nothing left to add, but when there
is nothing left to take away.*
ANTOINE DE SAINT-EXUPÉRY

Styrene Profiles

Material
styrene profiles

Tools
acrylic solvent / chopper / sanding bed / table saw

Tips & Techniques

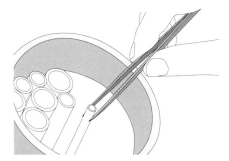

Arrange stock styrene profile parts horizontally to create a vertical three-dimensional skin pattern. Use a border guide, such as the ring shown here, to assemble elements into specific forms. Remove the guide when the glue is dry.

Applied Technologies & Alternate Methods
The styrene profiles block was made by hand out of machine-cut styrene elements. Patterns can also be created with a CNC mill or laser cutter, or by metal etching. You can carve a pattern onto a surface with a CNC mill, or laser-cut and -score a pattern onto planar layers, which can be stacked for depth. A pattern can also be etched into metal and be used as a guide for adding relief elements.

Architectural Concepts
convergence / exponential / figure/ground / fractal / haptic / interface / portal

Sample Model (p. 155)

Suggested Alternatives

Stereolithographic organic interior space

Basswood elements (p. 74)

Patterned styrene sheet (p. 30)

Stacked planes (p. 36)

Basswood screen (p. 26)

Architecture is inhabited sculpture.
CONSTANTIN BRANCUSI

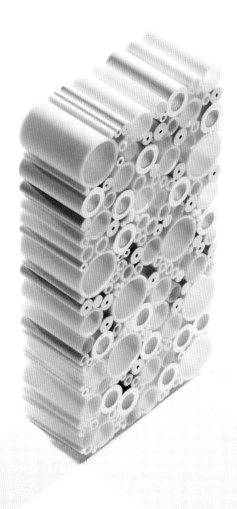

Saw-Cut Reveal

Material
basswood solid

Tools
drafting tools / table saw

Tips & Techniques

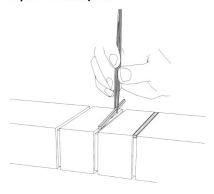

Inlay a different material in reveals to add detail and create surface differentiation.

Applied Technologies & Alternate Methods
The saw-cut reveal block was made in the machine shop and then notched with a table saw at equal intervals. Relief linework can also be created with 3-D printing/stereolithography, a CNC mill, or a laser cutter. Use a 3-D printer to print a form with a complex surface relief pattern, or rout a surface pattern into a solid with the CNC mill. A laser can also cut and score linework into material.

Architectural Concepts
detail / edge / line / modularity / pattern / reciprocal / subtractive

Sample Model (p. 156)

Suggested Alternatives

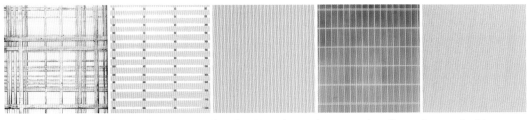

Saw-cut acrylic
(p. 44)

Basswood screen
(p. 26)

Generic patterned basswood

Laser-scored acrylic
(p. 60)

Basswood solid
(p. 18)

*Every motion of the hand in every one of its works
carries itself through the element of thinking, every
bearing of the hand bears itself in that element.
All the work of the hand is rooted in thinking.*
MARTIN HEIDEGGER

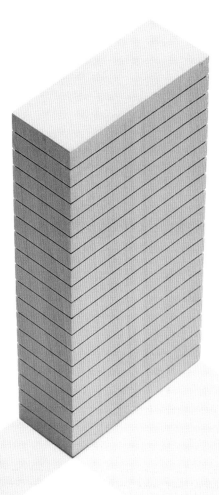

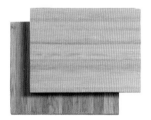

Acetate film

Acetate film is a thin, clear plastic with uniform optical properties and good dimensional stability. It is produced by two mechanical processes: forced extrusion and solvent casting. The latter produces a clearer, higher-quality product. In model building acetate film is commonly used to represent glazing and other transparent elements. The material, which tears easily and can be cut with a razor or an X-Acto knife, is available in clear and matte finish in sheets ranging from .003 to .020 inches in thickness. It can be printed with graphic and color information. Acetate works well when used in small areas structured by wall material, but ripples when spanning larger distances. It will flex to represent curvilinear glazing elements.

Acrylic

Acrylic, commonly known as Plexiglas, is a lightweight, rigid, synthetic material available in sheets, blocks, spheres, rods, and tubing. It comes in many varieties, including clear, transparent, translucent and opaque colors, and mirror-backed. The material can be processed using standard metal- or wood working tools, bonds easily using solvents or contact glues, can be heat-bent or pressure-formed, does not warp with changes in humidity, and, since it has no grain, does not require extensive filing and finishing. It is ideal for representing glazing but has the versatility to be used for virtually any modeling purpose. There are two types of acrylic: cell-cast and extruded. Extruded acrylic costs less, but melts when machined and scratches easily, while cast acrylic powders into dust when machined and is easily polished and finished.

Bamboo

Bamboo is a grass of the *Poaceae* family, characterized by its woody, hollow, round, straight, jointed stem. It is available in laminated sheets and planks that can range widely in density, at times achieving a strength three times that of oak. Bamboo veneer is a sustainable alternative to wood veneer.

Balsa wood

Balsa is the softest of all modeling woods and has a slightly shiny whitish surface. It is too weak to be structurally useful, but has an incredibly malleable form and can be cut, carved, bent, shaped, and bonded with great ease. It is best cut using an X-Acto knife and bonds well with cellulose cements or white glue. It is difficult to achieve a high level of finish with Balsa, as the surface is easily dented and its grained texture cannot be readily removed.

Basswood

Basswood is the preferred wood for almost all modeling purposes. It is light to reddish brown, and has a medium density, an indistinct, straight grain, and a uniform texture. Basswood is available in planks and sheets of various thicknesses, sheets with surface relief representing standard siding patterns, structural profiles, dowels, and solid chunks. It machines well, can be cut in any direction, sands easily, and achieves sharp edges without splintering. While a laser cutter will burn the cut edge, this can be sanded off for a cleaner presentation. The wood dries quickly with fairly high shrinkage but little warping and has good structural integrity when dry. In model building basswood is perfect for both structural framing and finish elements.

Bond paper

Bond paper is the ubiquitous white sheet stock typically made from eucalyptus pulp that is used in most offices and homes for electronic printing. Depending on the quality, it is a strong, durable paper with good absorption, erasability, and rigidity. Print digital scale elevations on bond paper and adhere it to chipboard to create a quick 3-D study model.

Brass

Brass is an alloy of copper and zinc that is frequently plated with chrome, nickel, or silver. Its reddish golden appearance is often indistinguishable from bronze. Brass is softer and more workable than steel; can be cut, bent, soldered, and cast fairly easily; and polishes to a high luster. The metal is available for modeling purposes in sheets, wire, tubing, and square, rectangular, and oval profiles. Brass is a standard material used for metal etching of model parts. Brass profile elements can also add structural integrity to model assemblies (paint the brass to match the model or building materials).

Cardboard

Cardboard is a gray-brown heavy-duty paper product made of ground wood pulp particles. It generally consists of a corrugated middle sandwiched between two flat faces, forming a relatively sturdy board that can be bent easily in one direction or cut with a knife. In model building cardboard is often used for structural support, to form large flat surfaces, or to create rough, fast topographic models of a site.

Cardstock

Cardstock is a paper product of medium thickness used for elements that require more durability than regular printing paper and more flexibility than cardboard. Adhere double-sided tape to one side of cardstock and flock the other to create flocked adhesive paper. Because of its thinness and stiffness cardstock is also a great material for templates.

Cement

Cement is a dry powder consisting of lime, silicon, aluminum, iron, and gypsum that when combined with water has adhesive and cohesive properties. For modeling purposes cement, which hardens in place, is typically used as a binder.

Cherry

Cherry is a rich, red-brown medium-density wood with a uniform, straight grain and a lustrous smooth texture. It is bendable and can easily be machined and surface-finished. The color of cherry wood can be used as a graphic accent in a basswood model. Cherry is available in model-scale lumber dimensions.

Chipboard

Chipboard is a processed material consisting of glued-together wood chips that is typically available in sheets of different plys or thicknesses. It is a dense, inexpensive product with a rough finish and a warm gray color. It forms curves when soaked in water and left to dry in a jig and tends to warp when exposed to excessive moisture. Chipboard cuts easily and can be machined and bonded in the same fashion as most unprocessed woods. Large-scale sheets are inexpensive and efficient for creating topographic models.

Copper

Copper is a soft, reddish-brown metal known for its properties of conduction. It is the basis of the alloys bronze and brass, and is the only metal that oxidizes in air, giving it a red or green patina. The metal is malleable, polishes well, and can be soldered and bonded easily. Copper sheeting and profiles can be processed with modeling tools and standard woodshop machines.

Cork

Cork sheeting is sourced from the outer bark of the *Quercus suber*, or cork oak tree, a species native to southwest Europe and northwest Africa. It is lightweight, impermeable, and easy to cut with a knife. Cork bonds well with thickened superglue and white glue, and is available in sheets and rolls of various colors, degrees of graining, and thicknesses. With its natural color, it makes a great material for topographic layers.

Foam core

Foam core consists of a thin sheet of polystyrene foam sandwiched between two sheets of heavy white paper. It is available in many different thicknesses and is an excellent choice for quick massing studies, mock-ups, and stacked topographic models. The material is easily cut and produces finer lines than cardboard, but it tends to warp and does not react well to some glues and paints. For best results, bond foam core with a high-quality spray adhesive.

Gatorboard

Gatorboard consists of a layer of rigid polystyrene foam core sandwiched between two pieces of resin-infused wood fiber. Although it is lighter than plywood, this multilayered fortification makes the material very difficult to cut, crush, or dent, though it can be machined using standard woodworking tools and forms sharp corners without shredding. It maintains a high load capacity and is moisture- and warp-resistant, with an excellent surface quality for presentation.

Ground foam

Ground foam, also known as flock, consists of soft urethane and is used in model building to create landscape elements, giving the impression of plant life. A diluted white glue solution brushed on in a glaze bonds ground foam to most materials. Flock comes in different grades from fine to rough and is available in most landscape colors.

Mahogany

Mahogany is a very hard tropical wood native to the West Indies and Central and South America, with a rich reddish-brown color and a glossy surface. It has a straight grain and relatively few natural imperfections, does not shrink significantly, and must be processed with power tools. Mahogany can be used as a graphic accent in a basswood model. It is available in model-scale lumber dimensions in most hobby shops.

Maple

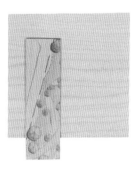

Maple is a hard, moderate-density wood native to North America and Europe with a light- to dark-brown color, a fine grain, and a uniform texture. It can be machined using standard woodworking tools and bonds easily with white glue. Similar in coloration to basswood, maple veneer can be used for modeling the site to achieve a completely monochromatic wood model.

Mat board

Mat board, also known as Bristol board, consists of a wood pulp board laminated between medium-grade white paper with a slick or matte finish. Mat board takes paint well and comes in a variety of thicknesses in 1- to 4-ply sheets. It has structural integrity, can be machined or cut with an X-Acto knife, and bonds with white glue.

MDF

MDF, or medium-density fiberboard, consists of a mixture of wood fiber and resin. It provides a uniformly flat surface with good structural integrity, comes stained in many different colors, and can be processed with standard woodworking tools. MDF is an inexpensive rigid sub-base material for site models.

Modeling clay

Modeling clay is a term that covers a group of malleable products used for sculpting and model building. All types of modeling clay can be sculpted, blended, and textured with standard modeling tools. Modeling clay can be used to quickly render organic forms for an experimental study.

Museum board

Museum board is an acid-free board made of 100 percent white cotton fiber. It flexes fairly easily in one direction but is quite stiff in the other due to the grain of the paper fibers. It is an expensive material with high finish quality that bonds well with white glue and can be cut easily with an X-Acto knife. Museum board is available in 2-, 4-, 5-, and 6-ply sheets in various shades.

Photopolymer

Photopolymer is a plastic that is kept in a liquid state and cures or becomes solid when exposed to light, usually emitted from a laser or lamp. It is the material commonly used in 3-D printing. Objects printed with photopolymers can be cut, sanded, and surface-finished.

Plaster

Plaster consists of white ground alabaster gypsum that is used for casting when mixed with water. In model building this material is useful for massing studies, producing smooth, precise forms, and uniformly duplicating specific building elements. Plaster absorbs moisture from the air and must be kept dry to properly harden. After curing, it can be cut, sanded, and carved with standard woodworking tools and machines.

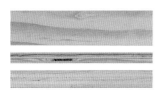

Plywood

Plywood consists of wood veneers glued together in a crosswise pattern, producing a lightweight, warp-resistant material. Aircraft plywood is made in sheets that come in thicknesses suitable for model making. It can be easily processed with regular woodworking tools, bonds well with white glue, and can withstand fasteners for joining. Plywood makes a good base substructure for models.

Polyurethane foam

Polyurethane foam is a resilient, flexible foam that takes paint and adhesives well due to its closed cell structure. It comes in densities from one to six pounds per cubic foot, ranging from very soft to semirigid. In model building this material can be used as a landscape base or a filler and is easily carved and formed using a sanding stick or other modeling tools. A pantograph (x-y-axes router) or CNC mill can cut foam topographic site models.

Resin

Resin is a clear liquid that can be found in trees or is synthetically manufactured and that cures with the use of a catalyst. It is soluble in alcohol, but not in water. Resin can be cast to represent translucent and transparent elements of the model, such as water. Resin powder is also used in 3-D printers, which first layer the powder and then a cure, such as CA (superglue).

Stainless steel

Stainless steel is a steel alloy with a mixture of chromium and nickel that is very strong and highly resistant to corrosion and rust. In model building it is useful for areas exposed to moisture and bonds well with all-purpose glues. Stainless steel can be chemically etched to create detailed model parts.

Styrene

This low-cost synthetic material, which comes in a variety of sheet thicknesses, rods, and profiles, is a good alternative to cardboard and is particularly useful for structural and curved elements of a model. It can be manipulated in a great variety of ways, is not sensitive to changes in temperature and humidity, cuts and sands easily, and finishes well due to its lack of grain. Styrene bonds with acrylic solvent, white glue, or superglue, and styrene extrusions curve without kinking.

Surface Finish

Numerous surface finishes exist, which are more or less effective depending on the base material in question. Acrylic urethane and primer are best for acrylic; waxes, oils, and wood stains work best with wood; latex paint is used for shelling foam; and clear coats produce a shiny finish on almost any material.

Task Board

Task board is a biodegradable model board with an edge that is identical to its surface. It machines and finishes well, is naturally rigid, and can be softened and formed using steam.

Veneer

Veneer is a thin layer of wood typically covering particleboard to convey the appearance of solid wood. Its characteristic grain is achieved by slicing through the growth rings of a tree at varying angles. For modeling purposes, veneer can be cut with an X-Acto knife and glued onto a structural backing using white glue or sheet adhesive. Paper-backed veneer will not split when surfacing curved forms.

Vinyl

Vinyl, also known as polyvinyl chloride or PVC, is a versatile, durable, inexpensive material made from polymerized vinyl chloride or vinyl acetate. It is a thermoplastic compound that can be reprocessed using heat and can be made flexible, rigid, or semiliquid. Vinyl veneers come in many colors, thicknesses, and surface finishes and can be laminated onto other materials and laser-cut or machined.

Walnut

Walnut is a hard, dark-brown wood with an open grain that can be machined with standard woodworking tools. It bonds easily with white glue, takes a high polish, is quite bendable, and has low shrinkage. Walnut wood is most commonly used in model making as a veneer.

Wire

Wire is a slender string of drawn metal used for modeling trees and small-scale structural elements. Wire is available in copper, steel, aluminum, and coated in plastic.

Acrylic solvent

Acrylic solvent is a clear, fluid glue designed for bonding polystyrene and PVC. The solvent works by melting the surface of the material, fusing the joint without adhesive residue. Temporarily hinging the joints together with tape allows the solvent to wick into the joint. Solvent is applied by loading an animal-hair brush with solvent from a pump dispenser.

Band saw

The band saw is a woodworking machine composed of a continuous, narrow band with cutting teeth driven by two wheels. It is ideally suited for curved, freeform cuts, stacked material cuts, and solid acrylic and wood cross sections. Band saws are usually oriented vertically, allowing the material to be fed horizontally into the mechanism.

Beanbag

Beanbags are small sacks typically filled with lead shot. They can be used as an alternative to clamps and come in handy for weighing down organic forms while adhesive-bonded parts are drying.

Belt sander

A belt sander is a hand-held or stationary one-directional sanding device consisting of an electric motor and a seamless loop of sandpaper mounted on a pair of turning drums. It is used to quickly remove material from large surfaces, and to trim and finish wood and other materials.

Bestine

Bestine is a versatile cleaner commonly used for thinning rubber cement. It is a nonstaining solvent that does not dissolve most plastics and will not remove most paints when cleaning surfaces. Paper templates that have been bonded with spray adhesive to materials can be removed with Bestine without leaving a blemish on the material.

Brillianize

Brillianize is a nontoxic, antistatic cleaner commonly used for cleaning and polishing acrylic. It can also be used on most other plastics as well as glass and metal. It is important to remove dust, dirt, and fingerprints from the interior surfaces of acrylic model parts before assembly. An antistatic will also prevent dust from being drawn to the surface of the acrylic.

Brush

A brush is a tool consisting of bristles or hair attached to a handle, used for painting, cleaning, polishing, and delivering solvent to adhere a joint. Animal-hair brushes are recommended for solvent, as solvents will dissolve synthetic bristles. Keep brushes away from superglue and clean them regularly.

Bubble level

Bubble levels are surface levels, which are useful to check model parts in relation to other parts and the site.

Bucket

A bucket is a watertight container used to hold and carry water and other liquids. In model making buckets are useful for mixing plaster, cement, and flocking, and for soaking wood you want to bend.

Buffer wheel

A buffer wheel is a round object propelled in circles by a motor used for polishing. Machined acrylic can be brought back to its polished state with a buffer wheel.

Burnishing tool

A burnishing tool is a rounded implement usually made of metal or bone, used for polishing metals, smoothing double-sided sheet adhesives, and applying transfer graphics.

Caliper

A caliper is an adjustable measuring instrument made of two legs attached to a central hinge used to make precise measurements of lines, diameters, and cross sections. Use calipers to transfer dimension from one object to another or from an object to a machine setting.

Carbon paper

Carbon paper is paper coated on one side with a layer of dry ink usually adhered with wax that is placed between an original document and a blank piece of paper. When pressure is applied to the original document, the dry ink of the carbon paper is transferred to the underlying paper to form a copy of the original document. Carbon paper can be used in model making to transfer scaled plotted information directly onto the material to be cut. For example, tape carbon paper to the back of a topographic map for a quick transfer of layer information onto sheet material.

Chisel

A chisel is a hand tool consisting of a metal cutting edge attached to a handle that is driven with a hammer or mallet in order to carve small pieces from hard material such as wood, stone, or metal.

Chopper

A chopper is a hand tool consisting of a razor blade attached to a metal arm that operates with a horizontal cutting motion. Guides can be used to make clean, reproducible cuts at 30-, 45-, 60-, and 90-degree angles. Styrene and basswood strip profiles are cleanly cut with a chopper.

Circle template

A circle template is a clear plastic sheet with different-sized holes that can be used as a pattern for drafting accurate circles and arcs.

Clamp

A clamp is a fastening tool typically made of wood or metal that is used to hold objects firmly in place while gluing, machining, or welding. Small-scale clamps are available for model making and can hold the model together, freeing both hands for work.

Compass

A compass is an instrument consisting of two legs, often holding a pen or pencil, joined by a movable hinge. It is used for measuring the distance between two points, indicating even spacing, and drawing circles.

Compressed air

A high-pressure canister containing air is used to blow dust and dirt out of small spaces in the model.

Contact cement

Contact cement is an all-purpose, water-resistant, quick-drying glue made of neoprene and naphtha or toluol. It has relatively low strength and is susceptible to deterioration, but it will bond on contact without clamping and works well as a quick adhesive for all foams, as well as plastic, rubber, glass, leather, metal, and veneer. For a strong bond, contact cement should be applied to both surfaces and allowed to dry before the objects are joined together. Contact cement is an effective adhesive for bonding large sheets of material.

Contour marker

A contour marker uses sliding slats and a snap lock to transfer specific curves from one object to another.

Copier

A copier makes quick, inexpensive reproductions of paper documents. In model building a copier is useful for quickly generating multiple templates for cutting.

Cotton cloth

A cotton cloth is a piece of fabric used to clean and polish objects during model making. Smooth cotton clothes do not leave fiber particles on the model parts as a paper towel or other fabrics might.

Cutting mat

A cutting mat is a smooth, semihard, durable piece of vinyl or rubber, often marked with a gridded cutting guide that is placed over finished surfaces to protect them while cutting. A cutting mat will not dull the blade of your knife as quickly as other hard surfaces. The surface of the mat heals after a cut is made.

Disc sander

A disc sander consists of a rotating, motor-driven disk with sandpaper attached and is used to grind and smooth surfaces. It is usually stationary and can include an adjustable workbench and edge guide. Select the diameter of the disc for the appropriate task at hand. Sand smaller parts of the model on a smaller-diameter disc sander.

Divider

A divider consists of a pair of compasses with pointed legs and is used for measuring precise distances, dividing line segments, scribing arcs and circles, and comparing the sizes of different drawing elements.

Double-sided tape

Double-sided tape is a moisture-resistant tape coated with adhesive on both sides, which is designed to instantly stick two lightweight surfaces together without buckling or warping them. Use double-sided tape to adhere small parts to welding blocks for disc sanding and cutting on the bandsaw, or as a final adhesive for sheet material and composite layering.

Drafting board

A drafting board is a smooth surface that provides backing support when drawing on flexible uneven surfaces. A drafting board has a parallel ruler attached to it for mechanical drafting.

Drafting pencil

A drafting pencil has a graphite lead core housed in a wood or metal casing. The lead comes in a variety of hardnesses and colors.

Drafting tools

This general term describes all implements that aid in the process of architectural drawing. Examples include compasses, scales, triangles, tracing paper, and pencils.

Dremel

A Dremel is a versatile, hand-held, electric rotary tool with interchangeable bits such as pin drills, grinders, sanders, and polishing wheels. The chucks are exchangeable to receive bits as thin as .5 mm. This is the most effective tool for making small precise holes.

Drill
A drill is a hand-held, motor-driven rotary tool used to make holes in wood, metal, concrete, and other materials.

Drill bit
A drill bit is the small metal attachment inserted into the chuck of a drill. Drill bits come in 1/32-inch increments from 1/16-inch to 3/4-inch and are produced in a variety of forms to accommodate specific materials and applications. Micro bits are available for model making.

Drill bit gauge
A drill bit gauge is a metal plate with different-sized circles that allows you to quickly identify the diameter of a drill bit or diameter of the drill bit needed by inserting the bit or the cylindrical part into a labeled, correspondingly sized hole.

Dust mask
A dust mask is a piece of fabric attached to the face with straps that covers the nose and mouth to prevent harmful particles from entering the respiratory system. Use a dust mask when the tools and materials you are using create airborne dust and particulate.

Earplugs
Earplugs are small pieces of moldable material that are inserted into the ears to prevent sound from entering. Use earplugs when working with tower pools to protect your ears.

File
A file is a metal, usually steel, tool with a rough, patterned surface used for reducing or smoothing the surfaces of metal, wood, and acrylic. Files useful for model making come in flat, round, square, and triangular cross sections with fine to course cuts.

Foam tape
Foam tape is a resilient, high-density, double-sided tape used for adhering cardboard and other lightweight materials and filling in the gaps between unlevel surfaces. Use foam tape to attach model parts to an extension stick for painting.

French curve
A French curve is a plastic, wood, or metal template used to draw smooth curves of varying sizes and shapes. The trace can be achieved with a drafting pencil or a knife.

Gloves

A glove is a close-fitting dressing for the hand used to protect the skin against harmful chemicals and abrasives. Wear gloves when working with acrylic. Machine-cut acrylic has edges that are sharp enough to slice skin. Gloves should also be worn to protect skin from chemicals such as Bestine.

Goggles

Goggles are protective eyewear typically made of rubber or plastic that fit snugly on the face and prevent harmful materials from entering the eyes. They can be worn over prescription eyeware. Wear goggles when sanding materials such as foam that create superfine particulate.

Grinder

A grinder is a power tool consisting of an abrasive wheel powered by a motor. The abrasive on the wheel's surface shears off small chips of material.

Hammer

A hammer is a pounding implement consisting of a metal head connected to a handle at a right angle used for driving nails and flattening materials. In model making the hammer is used to construct sub-bases and travel boxes.

Heat gun

A heat gun is a hand-held device resembling a hair dryer that emits a hot stream of air and is used for drying paint and adhesives or for softening thermoplastic materials such as acrylic.

Highlighter

A highlighter is a felt-tip pen that is used to draw attention to sections of documents by marking them with a vivid, translucent color. When working on a model the colors help focus on needed information located on the many drawings needed to make a model.

Hot glue

Hot glue is dispensed by pushing solid glue sticks through a trigger-operated glue gun. Hot glue dries almost instantly and is useful for quick crude mock-ups.

Hot wire cutter

A hot wire cutter consists of a thin, taut metal wire, which is heated and used to cut polystyrene foam. As the material to be cut approaches the wire, the heat from the wire vaporizes the foam. Use a hot wire cutter when making quick foam massing models ideal for urban context models for master planning.

Light table

A light table is a table or portable box with a built-in light source and a translucent white surface. Place drawings on the lit surface for easy tracing.

Machinist block

A machinist block is a metal block used to measure the accuracy of a right angle. Machinist blocks can also be used as weights or glued to a model part as an extension during machining.

Machinist square

The machinist square's primary use is checking the accuracy of a right angle. Adjustable squares have a steel blade pinned into a heavy body at 90 degrees. Checking and rechecking model parts during assembly will ensure the final assembled parts will be true.

Masking tape

Masking tape is a pressure-sensitive tape that is easy to remove, leaving little or no residue. Masking tape is rated on a 1–100 scale for its strength of adhesion. Most masking jobs for painting require a 50-range masking tape. When masking laser-scored parts, translucent masking tape can be helpful, such as rice paper tape. Masking tape can also be used to temporarily hold joints together during gluing and to tape down drawings.

Metal ruler

A metal ruler is the primary tool in model building for making straight cuts, scribes, and scores on sheet material. Plastic rulers will nick and aluminum rulers will dull your blades. A stainless steel ruler with etched 1/32-inch graduations is useful for transferring measurements from drawings to parts and from parts to machines.

Mold release

Mold release is a wax or polymer compound applied to the surface of a mold to create a barrier or seal to prevent the cast substance from adhering to the mold and allowing the model to easily eject from the mold.

Palm sander

A palm sander is a handheld power sander that works by vibrating in a circular pattern. It can be operated with one hand and can handle both rough and finish sanding jobs. When palm sanding wood, remember to sand with the grain.

Pliers

Pliers are used to grip, bend, cut, and hold objects, transferring the force of the hand's grip to the pinch of the pliers. Of the many types of pliers available, needle-nose and curved pliers are the most useful in model making.

Polishing cream

Polishing cream smoothes the surface of acrylic after machining it to a polished clear state. Polishing creams come in three strengths: heavy scratch remover, fine scratch remover, and shine and cleaner.

Red pencil

A pencil with red lead is a useful tool for marking model parts. The pencil marks are visible on most material and erasable. The eraser can also be used as a push stick for small parts on table saws with 4-inch blades.

Respirator

A respirator is a safety device worn over the mouth and nose that prevents dust and toxic fumes from entering the respiratory tract. Wear a respirator when working in the spray booth with paints or vaporous chemicals.

Rice paper tape

Rice paper tape is a thin and strong yellow masking tape that is made from rice plant fiber and covered with an acrylic adhesive. The tape is thin enough to produce sharp and edgeless painting lines, and its adhesive does not leave a residue. The translucent tape is ideal for masking laser-scored model parts for painting.

Roller

A roller is a hand tool with a rotating cylinder attached to a handle. Use a roller to smooth surfaces during lamination of sheet material to ensure a continuous bond.

Rubber mallet

A rubber mallet is a hammer with a large rubber head that will deliver a softer blow than a regular hammer. In model making rubber mallets are useful for pounding veneer into place.

Sanding bed

A sanding bed is a flat surface with an abrasive sanding texture. You can make your own sanding bed by applying a spray adhesive to a sheet of sandpaper and adhering it to a flat smooth surface.

Sanding stick

Sanding sticks are custom-made by the model maker to fit the sanding job, which will determine the stick's shape and size, and the grit of sandpaper. Choose the appropriate size and shape, then smoothly apply one layer of sandpaper with spray adhesive.

Sandpaper

Sandpaper is a paper with an abrasive coat on its surface, which can be used to level, shape, polish, finish edges, smooth surfaces, and remove burrs from material. Sandpaper is graded by a grit system numbered with high grits (360–600) for polishing, medium grits (80–220) for material removal and smoothing, and low grits (16–40) for course removal and smoothing. Sandpaper can be adhered to a sanding bed, sanding block, or sanding stick to achieve a plane surface, adhered to cylindrical form for curved surfaces, or used as a sheet (fold to stiffen).

Scale

A scale is a specialized ruler used to measure or translate dimensional information from reduced scale drawings. Most scales have a range of calibrated scales.

Scissors

Use scissors to cut paper, thin mat boards, metal etch, and other thin materials.

Scoring tool

A scoring tool, consisting of a hooked metal blade and a handle, is used together with a metal ruler to create scores for snapping material in two pieces, folding it, or generating detailed linework. Place the ruler along the line to be scored and drag the scoring tool along the edge to create a straight score line. Depending on the depth desired, repeat the score.

Screwdriver

Screwdrivers are used for driving a screw into a material or removing it from it. They are available for all screw head configurations and come in many sizes, including miniature for model building.

Sieve

A sieve is a hand tool with a metal mesh or perforated bottom used to separate coarse material from fine material or for straining and refining paint. Use a sieve when applying flocking (ground foam) to achieve an even carpeted surface coating.

Single-edged razor

Single-edged razors consist of a thin steel blade with one sharp edge and an edge designed for handling. In model making they are useful for detailing, trimming, cutting, scraping, and sanding.

Spackling paste

Spackling paste is a water-based filler that comes in various grades of coarseness. Use spackling paste to fill cavities and small holes in wood and other materials.

Spatula

Spatulas are long blunt metal blades with rounded or flattened ends. Their stiff flexibility makes them useful for delivering glue to a joint, separating glued surfaces, and applying fillers.

Spindle sander

A spindle sander is a sanding machine with a vertical oscillating cylindrical drum with a gritted sleeve. Spindle sanders can smooth marks on curved edges and on the inside surfaces of holes.

Spray adhesive

Spray adhesive is a sprayable glue that is available in different grades of adhesiveness, from low-tack to high-tack. Remountable spray adhesive is a low-tack adhesive that leaves little or no residue and can be readily removed from material. Higher-tack adhesives can be used as permanent bonds for sheet materials.

Spray gun

A spray gun is a high-volume, low-pressure (HVLP) paint gun used to deliver paints in small droplets mixed with air to achieve a thin even surface layer. It is particularly useful for model building, because the detail and fine linework on most model parts require a delivery of paint that dries fast and can be layered.

Stirring stick

Use wooden stirring sticks to stir stagnant paints and adhesives. They can also serve as extensions to which model parts can be attached during painting for easier handling.

Superglue

Superglue (CA or cyanoacrylate) is an ultra-thin-grade viscose adhesive that bonds with the aid of humidity. It works by wicking into tight-fitting joints by capillary action. The surfaces to be bonded must be held together, allowing superglue to seep into the joint. Regular superglue cures almost instantly, while thicker superglue cures in minutes, allowing for assembly time, and can be applied to a surface for bonding.

Superglue accelerator

Kicker or superglue accelerator polymerizes superglue. The presence of the vapor around the super-glued joint will instantly set the bond. Superglue can also be used as a filler when cured with baking soda.

Table saw

A table saw consists of a circular saw blade geared on an arbor run by a motor. Two fences—a longitudinal and a cross-cut fence—aid in cutting. Blades are available in varying diameters and teeth for different cuts and materials. Table saws are also available in different sizes, with the small 4-inch table saw being best for the model maker.

Tape measure

A tape measure is a long flexible (and sometimes retractable) strip of metal or cloth marked with dimensional subdivisions used for measuring.

Template

A template is a pattern or mold used as a guide to cut or mold model parts. Templates can be cut out of scaled drawings, or they can be tracings of space, objects, or laser-cut shapes. They can be made of paper, vinyl, or any rigid and thin material.

Tracing paper

Tracing paper is a transparent paper that comes in rolls. When layered over a drawing, visual and dimensional information can easily be traced off the original drawing.

Triangle

A triangle is a drafting tool used for drawing lines at specific angles and for leveling and squaring model parts during assembly. Most are made of transparent plastic and are available in 90-45-45, 30-60-90, or adjustable degrees and come in different sizes. Triangles can also be used to check the settings on table saws, and belt and disc sanders.

Tweezers

Tweezers are a holding tool consisting of a compound metal lever. They allow the model maker to hold and pick up small objects and come with many different points that work well for model making, such as needle, curved, straight, and flat.

Vacuformer

A vacuformer is a simple machine that heats a sheet of polystyrene to forming temperature, places it onto a single surface mold, and holds the form by applying a vacuum between the mold surface and the sheet. Vacuformed molds can be used directly as model parts or as molds to cast objects from other materials, such as plaster or resin.

Vise

A vise is a gripping tool used to hold or clamp an object so work can safely be performed on it with tools such as drills, saws, sanders, and planes. The vise also frees up your other hand to use or steady tools.

White glue

White glue is an emulsion of water and copolymer polyvinyl that bonds wood, cork, and veneer. White glue dries clear, matte, and quickly. Diluted with water, it can be used to create a thin film of adhesive.

Wire cutters

Wire cutters are a mix between scissors and pliers. Their jawlike cutting edges are used to cut wire, wire mesh, and small metal etch parts.

Wrench

Wrenches are tools used for turning nuts and bolts. They are available in various sizes and types. Use a wrench when securing a model to a base by bolting the core to the underside of the base.

X-Acto knife

The X-Acto knife is a hand-held utility knife with interchangeable blades mounted in a penlike body. X-Acto knives are used for cutting, chiseling, sawing, punching, and routing. The cutting blade most frequently used in model making is the #11 blade. The chisel blades come in handy for scraping, punching out metal etch parts, and carving out material. Change the blade frequently for a precise and clean cut.

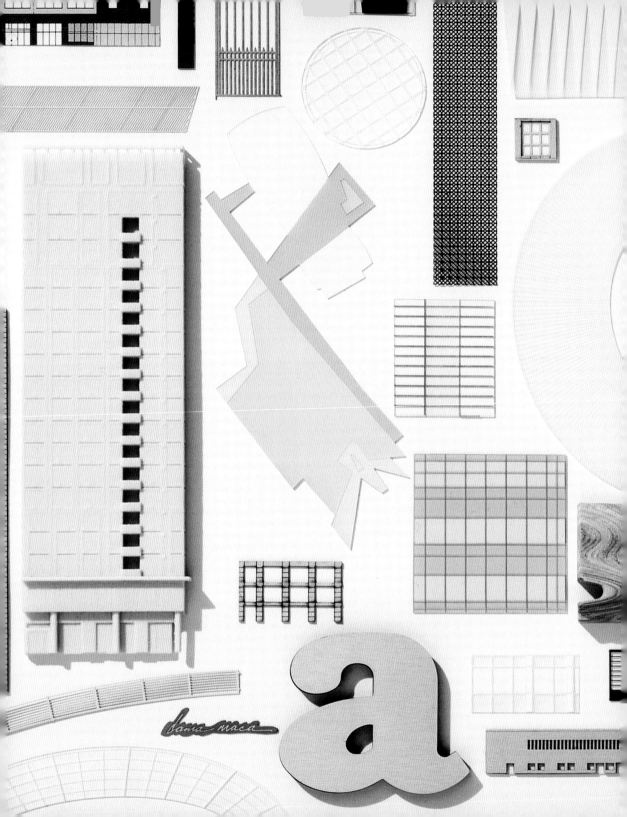

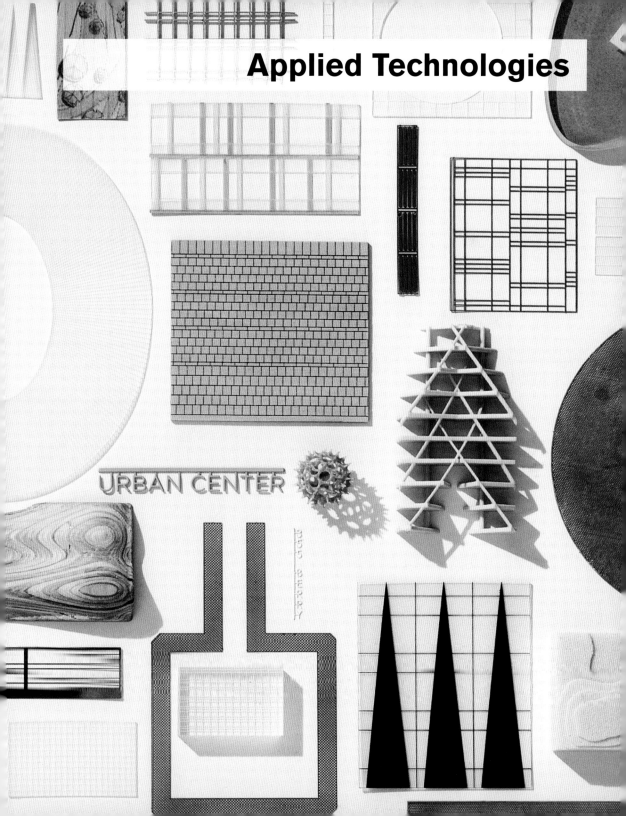

Applied Technologies

3-D Printing

3-D printing is an additive fabrication technology that produces physical objects directly from three-dimensional CAD models. Following the concept of layered manufacturing, the 3-D printer slices a CAD model into thin cross-sectional layers. The physical form is created as the machine prints and stacks each layer successively by first depositing a fine coat of powder material and then binding it with a light spray of superglue adhesive from an inkjet printhead. Typically, each layer is about .1 mm thick, and the x-y resolution is similar to that of a laser printer.

Materials
Powder with a superglue binder. The powder can consist of various materials, such as plaster, corn starch, resin, or wood.

Appropriate Use
A 3-D printer is most effective for modeling during the conceptual design stage, when a rough surface finish and slight dimensional imprecision (due to the printer's relatively low resolution) do not matter. 3-D-printed objects can be used to visualize complex forms (especially those with complex internal spaces), to explore spatial relationships, or to create multiple identical objects. Once printed, a form cannot be manipulated without compromising its structural integrity and surface finish.

Acid Etching

Acid etching is a subtractive process that allows for the transference of a two-dimensional graphic onto a metal plate. First the artwork or drawing is made into a negative on photographic film. The design is then transferred, by exposure to ultraviolet light, onto a metal plate prepared with coats of light-sensitive photo resist. The sheet is then treated with acid, which eats away at the unprotected negative space. Etching can be done all the way through the material to create a punch, or at a controlled depth, resulting in a relief or surface score. A metal etching service will require a digital file of the graphic or dimensioned drawings. Vector files are best, but raster image files can also be used, including grayscale photographs. Acid-etched parts come in a sheet tree, attached by small tabs for easy removal.

Materials
Brass, bronze, nickel, stainless steel, copper, silver, mild steel

Appropriate Use
Due to its material strength, structural integrity, and dimensional precision, acid-etched metal is most useful for producing ultrathin (0.001–0.062-inch), detailed model parts that may not be possible to fabricate using a laser. Though whole facades can be etched in metal, the process is indispensible for depicting details such as screens, railings, furniture, foliage, and trellises. If necessary, etched metal can be painted to represent a variety of materials.

CNC Milling

CNC milling is a subtractive fabrication technology in which a computer uses a CAD file to guide a milling machine to cut away material in order to create a complex physical object. Typically, a CNC mill consists of a table, on which the material is placed and moved in the x-y-axes, and a tool spindle that bores into the material on the z-axis.

Materials
Wood, plywood, MDF, cast acrylic, and, in sheet form, aluminum, brass, steel, and stainless steel

Appropriate Use
CNC milling is a great technology for creating geometrically complex and organic forms in relief, using a wide range of materials. This can be useful both for modeling structures and site topography. CNC milling makes fabricating multiple, identical parts and master molds, from which parts can be cast, easy. The CNC mill can also be used to engrave complex patterns onto material.

Laser

A laser (short for Light Amplification by Stimulated Emission of Radiation) is a prototyping tool that precisely cuts and scores a variety of planar materials on the x- and y-axes. Using a 2-D CAD file as a guide, the laser focuses an intense beam of infrared light or heat onto a precise point to melt, vaporize, or burn off the material and, in turn, create a cut or score on the surface. You can optimize your drawings for laser-cutting and -scoring by observing some of the following tips: Differentiate materials and types of cuts and scores by locating the information on different layers. Make sure there are no duplicate or overlapping lines; these will cause the laser to cut in the same place multiple times, yielding an undesirable result. For high-tolerance parts, offset the linework to be cut by the laser beam width. For most materials a .004-inch offset is sufficient. The space between cut lines should be equal to material thickness. Use polylines.

Materials
All materials with a low thermal conductivity and reflectivity can be cut and scored with a laser. Model making materials include acrylic, basswood, plywood, paper, and vinyl.

Appropriate Use
A laser is most useful when extremely precise cuts are necessary, which would be hard to achieve by hand or using traditional shop machines. It is an effective tool for creating multiple planar parts (such as floor plates), and complicated facades with many apertures and surface texture, as well as for sites that depict complex patterning or circulation. Laser scores can also be helpful guides during model construction.

Printing/Plotting

A peripheral to a computer, a printer/plotter uses a digital file to produce a hard copy document on a variety of materials. Inkjet printers are the most common and function by depositing droplets of ink onto the material.

Materials
Printers and plotters are able to print on paper, cardstock, acetate, and other thin materials, such as wood veneer.

Appropriate Use
Printed documents are indispensible for use as templates and for transferring information from hard copy to modeling material. Printed images can also be applied directly to the model to add color and line information to facades, sites, or glazing. You can also build quick mock-ups using printed cardstock.

Stereolithography

Stereolithography is an additive fabrication technology that produces physical objects directly from three-dimensional CAD models. Like 3-D printing, stereolithography uses a layering process. The machine deposits a layer of liquid UV-curable photopolymer resin onto a platform and a UV laser traces a pattern onto the liquid, curing the resin. The machine continues to deposit and cure the resin to form each successive layer. Stereolithography requires the use of support structures that are automatically generated during the print, but must be manually removed once the print is complete.

Materials
UV-curable photopolymer resin

Appropriate Use
Stereolithography is most useful for modeling complex, organic forms with elaborate internal spaces. The process is also effective for creating identical multiples and master molds for casting parts in other materials. Objects created with stereolithography (photopolymers) can be machined and surface-finished.

Best Practices & General Tips

- Modeling supplies and tools are available in hobby shops, hardware stores, and specialty art supply stores. Be resourceful: scrap and cut-offs of materials make great modeling materials.

- The general safety rules of a woodshop apply to model making at your studio desk.

- Work in a well-ventilated studio space.

- Organize your workstation. Keep a box for model parts and locate your tools for easy access. Stack materials.

- Work on a flat, smooth, nonporous surface such as granite or glass. Most glues will not adhere to granite or glass.

- Ask a series of questions before starting: Who will the audience be? What design concept do you want to embed in the model? What purpose will the model serve? What would you like to investigate? Are you making a study model, a fundraising model, a presentation model, a conceptual model, or a planning model?

- Plan ahead and schedule back from the deadline. Set rigid deadlines and plan for delay. Don't forget to schedule drying times for paint and glue.

- Engineer the model for structural integrity. Draw the thicknesses of model material in section to begin this process. Take standard material thicknesses into consideration when designing the model assembly.

- Always plot a set of drawings at model scale.

- Investigate materials and tools to ensure you are selecting the most appropriate for the desired outcome. Each method of fabrication has tolerances dictated by your choice of material and technology.

- Test and sample techniques, finishes, palettes, and materials before getting started.

- Pay attention to the order of operations. First fabricate, assemble, and surface-finish individual parts. Then combine parts to compose the whole model.

- Plan a spray-paint timeline that is merged with the assembly plan when building a model with multiple colors. Spraying parts as smaller unicolor assemblages will avoid difficult and time-consuming masking and provide a cleaner paint result.

- Always have a tool between your hand and the model (tweezers, brush, knife, spatula).

- Clamps and vises make a great third hand. Always work with both hands and hold the object in place with clamps, a vise, double-stick tape, or weights.

- Custom-make tools for specific tasks.

- Always cut extra parts when creating multiples. Mishaps can occur at any step (sanding, finishing, painting, assembly) of the process.

- Detailed parts take more time. Do not work on these parts at the expense of the completion of the model.

- Review books and online sources for additional tips and techniques.

Assembly

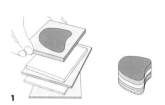

Assembly: mass/composite

▶ Create a solid form from sheet materials. Select a thickness that relates to the scale or architectural pattern of the project (floor-to-floor heights, slabs, window openings, grid, etc.). Stacking a series of horizontal sections is also a quick way to mass out complex organic forms. **①**

▶ Stack gatorboard plates to create a solid core that can be machined into shape and sheathed.

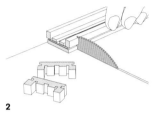

▶ Laminate stacked sheets of cork together to create a solid. Note that stacked material will have a cumulative measurable dimensional error.

▶ Create a pattern by layering different materials in a stacked solid.

▶ Bond simple profile elements together to create a complex mass extrusion profile of a desired footprint. Slice the profile into multiple uniform parts as needed using a small-blade table saw. **②**

Assembly: screen/detail

▶ Create a three-dimensional louver relief by etching a louver pattern into a stainless-steel plate. Leave small connector tabs to the left and right of the louvers and then twist the louver elements into position with tweezers. Half-etching the metal along the fold lines allows for easy and precise folding. **③**

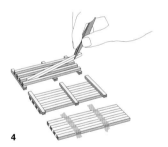

▶ Create modulated complex structural elements by using styrene and basswood profiles cut into uniform lengths. Cutting the profiles slightly longer than needed will allow you to sand them after assembly to create an even line. Arrange the strips on a flat surface, alternating basswood with styrene (with no space in between), and hold them in place with a weight (such as a metal square). Tape the assemblage together and flip it over. Glue two or more basswood elements perpendicular to the strips with white glue, holding them down with a weight to mitigate warping. Let dry before removing the tape and styrene spacers. When making a styrene screen use basswood spacers and solvent as the adhesive instead of white glue. **④**

Assembly: extrusion/parts

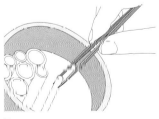

▶ Arrange stock styrene profile parts horizontally to create a vertical three-dimensional skin pattern. Use a border guide such as the ring shown here to assemble elements into specific forms. Remove the guide when the glue is dry. **⑤**

▶ Create stock patterns to ensure parts will be uniform throughout the model.

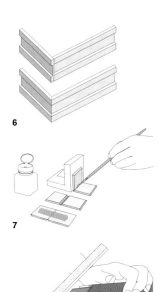

6

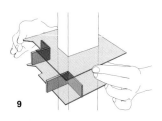

7

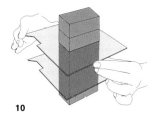

8

Assembly: joints

▸ Match patterns at the joint to create a consistent look. Matching a relief-patterned sheet material around a corner requires a beveled edge joint. Bevels can be hand-sanded on a 45-degree jig or routed on a machine. **6**

▸ Polish the beveled edges of acrylic to achieve a cleaner joint. Temporarily hinging the edges together with tape will also aid in a clean glue joint. Polished edges can be achieved through wet/dry sanding or flaming the edges with heat. When working with polished edges, use acrylic solvent adhesive, delivered with an animal-hair brush. **7**

▸ Use straight pins to hold parts together temporarily while glue is drying.

▸ Sand miters with a 45-degree jig and a sanding stick. **8**

Assembly: stack

▸ Stack floor-to-floor plates to create an armature for skins. For added structural integrity, thread columns through the stacked plates.

9

▸ Assemble acrylic floor plates using spacer jigs equivalent in size to the floor-to-floor dimension of your model minus the thickness of material used for the floor plate. The spacer jigs can be made out of gatorboard and are more stable if they have an L-shape. Thread a styrene column through the plate holes and glue the plates to the column before removing the spacer jigs. **9**

▸ Use a drill press to bore column holes through a stack of plates. The drill bit will sand the inner surface of transparent acrylic. To drill a transparent hole in acrylic, first drill a pilot hole (a smaller hole than desired), fill it with wax, and drill it to the desired dimension. The wax will polish the inner surface while you are drilling.

10

▸ To allow for an easy assembly of stacked floor plates, cut a core hole into the plates and use a core column with pre-scored floor-to-floor lines. **10**

▸ Create perimeter column holes in floor plates by assembling a stack of plates and cutting reveals into the stack on the table saw.

▸ Alternate acrylic (representing floor-to-floor space) with basswood (representing floor plates) to create a massed scaled solid for small-scale urban models.

▸ Stack formed laser-cut acrylic or basswood sections to sculpt complex organic shapes. **11**

11

Bend

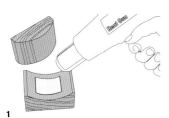

▸ Create organic acrylic shapes with planar acrylic through heat bending. Make a template of the desired curve and cut and sand negative and positive wood molds. Offset the molds by the thickness of the acrylic material. Span the flat acrylic sheet across the negative curved wood mold and apply heat with a heat gun in an even fashion. Place (do not press) the positive curve mold on top of the acrylic once it has dropped or bent into the negative curve position. Allow the wood mold to pull the heat out of the acrylic part. Remove the negative mold and let the acrylic rest on the positive mold. Be prepared to make multiple parts and select the best. **1**

▸ Create templates for complex forms by unwrapping the shape in CAD.

▸ Divide complex forms into a series of manageable curves for heat bending. Then reassemble.

▸ Vacuform clear polystyrene to create organic or complex glazing elements.

▸ Etched metal can easily be bent and curved using form molds. To fold metal, create fold lines by half-etching the metal. Etched metal can be readily bent and curved.

▸ Score mat board in successive, evenly spaced lines to create a segmented curvilinear plane. The scores will release the surface tension on one side of the board, allowing it to curve in one direction.

▸ Bend basswood by lightly soaking precut strips in water. Tape the dampened basswood to a curvilinear form matching the desired curve. Make sure to cover all of the basswood with tape to allow it to dry evenly without warping. **2**

Bond

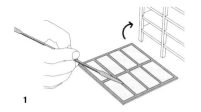

▸ Always use the least amount of glue possible to reduce drying time and to keep the surfaces of model parts clean.

▸ Do not deliver glue directly from the container. Deposit a small amount on a palette and apply it to the model part using a spatula or brush.

▸ Use an animal-hair brush to deliver solvent to an acrylic joint. Solvent will melt synthetic brushes.

▸ Polish all acrylic machine edges for a cleaner joint.

▸ Tape joints on the outside to hold them in place during gluing.

▸ Dilute white glue by 50 percent to create a thinner surface film when dry.

▸ Spray-painting interior surfaces is an easy method to conceal glue marks when working with acrylic. Spray the pattern of the glue joint onto the acrylic in a color similar to the color of the structure you wish to adhere. Apply glue to the sprayed surface pattern and adhere the structure to the acrylic. ❶

▸ Conceal glue marks on printed acetate by designing the glue seam as an opaque surface.

▸ Superglue will craze or fog acrylic unless a superglue accelerator is used directly after delivering the glue to the joint. Apply superglue accelerator to a small bit of paper towel and wave the vapors around the joint.

▸ Create basswood sheets by laminating 4-by-24-inch basswood planks together along the manufacturer's edge with white glue. Tape the edges and weigh down the board across the entire surface until the glue has dried. ❷

▸ Adhere different materials together with double-stick tape to create a composite solid to further sculpt and cut.

Cut

- ▸ For a crisp cut always use a metal ruler as a guide. Plastic rulers and triangles will be chipped by your knife, and the cut will not be straight.

- ▸ Always stand when you cut to exert the maximum pressure on the straight-edge and knife.

- ▸ Cut acrylic, styrene, and basswood with a sharp X-Acto knife, a metal edge ruler, and a cutting mat. Cut acrylic and styrene by scoring the surface and snapping the score across a table edge.

- ▸ Wood is easier to cut along the grain. Examine the wood and plan to cut along the grain.

- ▸ When creating a topography model using a CNC mill, cut negative and positive forms separately to seamlessly join when assembled. ①

1

1

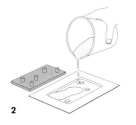

2

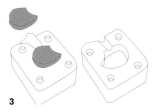

3

4

Mold

▸ Pour several identical parts by making a mold from an original object.

▸ Choose the method of fabrication of the mold depending on the material of the model part and the complexity of the form.

▸ Use CNC machines and 3-D printers to create precise master molds or vacuform a negative of the desired object.

▸ Create a continuous barrier seal on the mold. Its surface should be smooth and free of crevices, undercuts, and irregularities that might interfere with the separation of the object from the mold. Depending on the material used to create the mold, a release should be applied to the surface. Releases for molds range from specific sprays to household agents such as oil soap, Vaseline, and cooking oil spray. ①

▸ Vacuformed polystyrene shells are ready to use as molds. Rarely does an undercut exist in a vacuformed mold, increasing the chance of successful release of the object from the mold. When creating a vacuformed mold, make sure to elevate the positive object to be vacuformed to keep the styrene from wrinkling at the corners. The excess material can be trimmed off. ②

▸ Objects created through stereolithography can also be used as molds to translate precise forms into other materials such as resin, plaster, or porcelain. For example, you can use a photopolymer print to create a plaster mold for slip-casting multiple identical porcelain objects. ③

▸ Cast identical plaster model parts, and slowly sift the appropriate amount of plaster powder into a bucket of water by hand, until an island of plaster has formed. Mix water and plaster by hand or drill mixer until it is smooth and consistent, before pouring the mix into the mold. ④

▸ Create a cavity or add foam as a core in large plaster pours to reduce weight and material waste.

▸ Reinforce plaster and concrete molds with foam or wire structure.

Sand

1

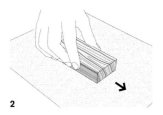

2

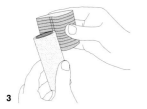

3

4

- ▸ Sand to accuracy; rarely cut to accuracy.
- ▸ Always sand with the grain. ②
- ▸ Create custom sanding sticks for specific jobs.
- ▸ Hand-sand concave forms by creating a tube or rod sanding stick. ③
- ▸ Sand concave extruded forms on the spindle sander.
- ▸ Create a smooth and semiaccurate grade in a topographic model through cutting and sanding. Modify the scaled topographic drawing by offsetting the topographic lines to create cut lines that reflect the excess material needed to sand back to the original contour lines. Lightly trace the original lines on the cut topographic planes, stack the layers, and palm-sand them back to the original lines. ④

Scale

▸ Use readymade entourage, such as people and cars, to add scale to a model.

▸ Linework (drawn, laser-cut, or printed) can indicate scale. For example, an element such as a curb, a paving pattern, or parking lines immediately adds scale to a model.

▸ Stepped topography provides scale and dimension to a site. Laminating the sides of a stepped base can create the illusion that the ground was carved from one block of material.

▸ Metal-etched parts add a level of detail and scale to a model that cannot be achieved through laser-cutting or machining.

▸ Cut styrene profiles and reassemble them to create small-scale detail elements.

▸ Add graphic scale to a three-dimensional model with printed paper and acetate.

▸ Add scale, material appearance, and graphic differentiation through surface finishes.

▸ In a scale model, grain structure will be read as graphic information. Avoid knots and blemishes, and consider the dimension of the grain when selecting wood.

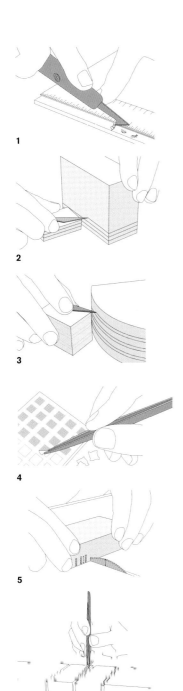

1

2

3

4

5

0

Score

- Use score lines as registration guides, masking guides, and assembly guides.

- Score thin material to create a precise fold line.

- Use a scoring tool when you want to remove a considerable amount of material, and an X-Acto knife to lightly score linework. ●1

- Score acrylic with floor-to-floor glazing and building patterns to create a quick schematic study.

- Hand-score acrylic with an X-Acto knife and a scoring tool or a surface gauge. Creating your own hand-scoring tool will help you achieve even score lines. Cut a number of acrylic squares in a thickness that matches the desired dimension between scores. The quantity of cut squares should be equal to the height of the entire score pattern when stacked (or half the height if the object you are scoring can be flipped). Adhere an X-Acto blade to one of the acrylic squares. On an even surface, slide the acrylic square with the dull side of the blade along the vertical surface of the object to create a score. Add an acrylic square to the bottom of the stack and repeat until your score pattern is complete. This is a great technique for applying scores to curvilinear model parts. ●2 ●3

- Create patterns on a facade by scoring a 2-ply mat board and peeling off the outer thin paper layer to reveal the inner chipboard core. You can draft the patterns directly on the object by hand or adhere a plot or print with low-tack adhesive to provide a template for scoring. Use a metal ruler as a score guide for your X-Acto knife. ●4

- You can also create score lines with a CNC mill laser, or by etching metal. The CNC will rout a reveal line, while the laser can score linework into a variety of materials. The process of half-etching generates a score line in metal (the full etch creates a void).

- Rub latex paint into a laser-scored line or a half-etched score on metal to emphasize the scored linework.

- Create a reveal in a solid material with the table saw by adjusting the height of the saw blade to match the depth of the desired reveal. Consider the blade thickness when notching, as this will determine the width of the reveal. Rotate the object to cut a continuous reveal. ●5

- Inlay different material in reveals to add detail and create surface differentiation. ●6

Site

- Print out satellite maps merged with topographic information to create topographic models with additional site information.

- Laser-cut and -score hardscape and landscape information into the base material to give context to a site and building.

- Cut topographic layers in a uniform base dimension. The edges of the base will serve as a registration line during assembly.

- When setting boundaries on a site model, consider the location of three-dimensional objects and their predominant colors. They must be visually balanced to provide a composed frame of view.

- Apply lichen or deer moss to add greenery to a site model.

- Twist bundles of copper wire to create tree trunks that can be manipulated into tree profiles. 1

- Represent trees conceptually using bare rods. This method gives a sense of wooded space without interfering with visibility. You can also create trees by stacking layers of cut paper onto thin rods.

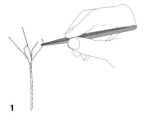

1

Surface

Surface: texture

▸ To create a polished acrylic form, cut or sculpt acrylic into the desired shape. Sand it with dry sandpaper (150–220 grit) and wet/dry sandpaper (220–800 grit) until scratches become cloudy or frostlike in appearance. Polish the object with heavy scratch remover cream, followed by fine scratch remover cream, then clean it with antistatic cleaner and a clean cotton cloth. ①

▸ A polished appearance on acrylic can also be achieved by spraying a sanded (220-grit) acrylic surface with a layer of clear coat.

▸ Laser-cutting acrylic results in polished edges.

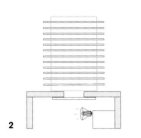

▸ Sanding acrylic creates a translucent surface that can add depth and aid in light transmission. Use a sanded acrylic core threaded through the model and base to transmit light from below the base, illuminating the model. Light leaks can be addressed with black tape or by spraying surfaces black or silver surrounding the core and under the base. ②

▸ Spraying unfinished acrylic with Dulcote (frost) creates a sanded or translucent appearance.

▸ Sand a foam stepped topographic site base cut on a pantograph or CNC machine to create a smooth graded surface.

▸ Sculpt cork with tweezers and a wire brush to achieve a textured surface to describe site conditions.

Surface: veneer

▸ Wood veneer or other thin materials can be adhered to a core form with numerous adhesives (depending on the materials used). A quick and effective adhesion method is double-sided tape. Cover the entire surface with adhesive to avoid buckling. ③

▸ When applying veneer, make sure to match the veneer in grain pattern, grain direction, and coloration of wood.

▸ Alternate the grain direction of the veneer for graphic pop and contrast. In an urban scale model the different grain directions can imitate road and curb conditions. ④

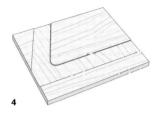

▸ Veneer the end grain on a wood massing block to create a monochromatic appearance.

▸ Apply a thin adhesive vinyl to acrylic to add graphic color or represent building material. Vinyl-coated acrylic can be laser-cut.

▸ Adhere paper prints of rendered elevations to a core form to create a quick three-dimensional model. Add shadows to the rendered elevations to create the illusion of depth.

5

6

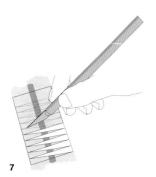

7

Surface: paint/color

▸ Always sand and prime material to create a paint-ready surface.

▸ Handle an object for painting by adhering it with foam double-stick tape to an extension stick (such as a paint stirring stick). This allows you to spray all surfaces but one in one go without touching the object. Wait for the paint to dry and cure, then flip the object over to spray the final surface. **5**

▸ When spray-painting multiple parts on one surface, adhere the parts with foam tape to a larger board for an efficient spray.

▸ When painting stock parts, be sure to spray-paint them at the same time to ensure consistent colors and surfaces.

▸ Add texture, graphic color, or building material representation by applying paint to model surfaces.

▸ Apply transparent color to acrylic by adding a tint to a clear coat and spray-painting the acrylic.

▸ Add color, scale, and linework to transparent glazing by overlaying colored acetate sheets with planar acrylic. **6**

▸ Adhesives can react with paint and create a blemished surface. Mask material for painting with tape that leaves little or no adhesive on the surface, such as rice paper tape or other masking tape.

▸ To create a quick mask for painting acrylic, laser-score the paint pattern into the acrylic, leaving the manufacturer's protective paper mask attached. After scoring, peel the mask from the desired opaque surfaces and leave areas representing glazing masked. You can also mask a laser-scored acrylic part by using the laser scores as cut guides for rice paper tape. The X-Acto blade easily slips into the score groove, guiding the blade along the score for a perfect mask outline of the desired pattern to be painted. **7**

▸ Represent water by spray-painting the interior surface of acrylic. Depth can be rendered by selecting the appropriate material dimension. The thicker the acrylic, the deeper it will appear.

▸ Stain basswood with thinned acrylic urethane for a better finish. Thinned urethane will evaporate and leave a thin film of color to seep into the wood. Regular wood stains will pick up the surface irregularity of basswood.

▸ Block light leaks with black or silver paint.

▸ Apply latex paint to a foam base to create a nonporous surface for adhering material layers and flocking.

▸ To speed up the drying and curing of a painted surface, place the painted part under a heat lamp or a lamp with an incandescent bulb for a low level of heat.

▸ When building a multicolored model, plan the assembly of parts based on their paint colors. The transition between colors is cleaner when objects are sprayed before assembly.

▸ Divide a stereolithography print into separate surface finish parts, spray on the color finish, and assemble.

Surface: flock

8

▸ Flock areas with ground foam to represent landscape. Adhere double-sided tape as a continuous surface to the back of green cardstock. To ensure it will stay flat, tape the perimeter to a piece of wood or a tabletop surface with the (unpeeled) double-stick side facing down. Brush a thin glaze of diluted white glue (approximately 1:1 dilution with water) onto the top of the cardstock. Sift the ground foam through a sieve until the surface of the cardstock is no longer showing visible glue or dampness. The drying time varies, but twenty-four hours is recommended. Gently vacuum or brush off extra ground foam once the glue has dried. If the flock is spotty, repeat the process. **8**

▸ Paint the surface of an object to be flocked in a color that is similar to the flock color.

▸ The coloration and texture of cork make it a natural background site color when flocked with ground foam.

▸ If landscape pads are irregular, flock sheets of material and then laser-cut them into appropriate shapes. Inversely, you can first cut the pads and then flock and adhere them to the model. Make sure to flock complex shapes in manageable sections and timeframes.

▸ Flock surfaces with sand using the same technique as for applying ground foam.

▸ Flock wire frame tree profiles to create the illusion of leaves or vines.

1

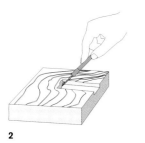

2

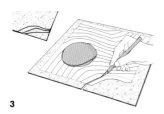

3

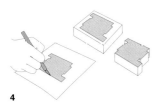

4

Template

▸ Use laser scores on the model facade as a template to assemble relief elements. Styrene profile parts can be cut and adhered to laser-scored linework to express exterior elements, structure, and sunshades. **1**

▸ Half-etch assembly guides in metal when creating small-scale precise relief elements such as screens, trellises, and structure.

▸ Apply relief elements to a plot or print using the printed linework as a guide.

▸ Use jigs as guides when assembling three-dimensional model parts.

▸ Insert a building into a topographic base by using its footprint as a template for cut lines.

▸ Sculpt foam with hand tools such as chisel blades, small metal spatulas, X-Acto knives, or scrapers to inlay roads, buildings, and landscape elements. If you have removed too much foam, make a filler patch with ground foam and white glue. **2**

▸ Adhere carbon paper to the back of a topographic map to transfer it onto sheets of material for cutting out individual topographic layers.

▸ You can also transfer topographic information by placing a plotted grading plan directly onto a sheet of cork or other material. Weigh down the drawing with beanbags so it does not move. Starting with the lowest grade, cut directly through the paper and cork, following the line to the edge of the base border to allow for a more precise registration during assembly. Move the grading plan onto an uncut cork sheet to cut out the next topographic layer and repeat until all topographic layers have been cut out. Stack the topographic layers and glue them together in sets of two, then sets of four layers, etc., to assure precise registration. **3**

▸ Create a complex solid by extruding the two-dimensional footprint of the desired form. Cut out a paper template from a print, plot, or hand drawing and adhere it with double-stick tape or a spray adhesive to a block of solid material (wood, acrylic, foam, stacked, composite). Roughly carve the shape with the band saw as described by the outline of the template, then sand it to achieve the accurate form. This is also a great way to make identical planes. Stack planes with double-stick tape and follow the instructions above. Then pry them apart with a thin metal ruler. **4**

5

6

▸ Adhere black-and-white templates of elevations and plans to mat board with a low-tack spray adhesive. Cut out the scale elevations and assemble them into a three-dimensional form. Peel off the black-and-white template prints and replace them with rendered color elevations for the final presentation. **5**

▸ Create seamless fitted parts (positive/negative) by using one form as a physical template to make the other. **6**

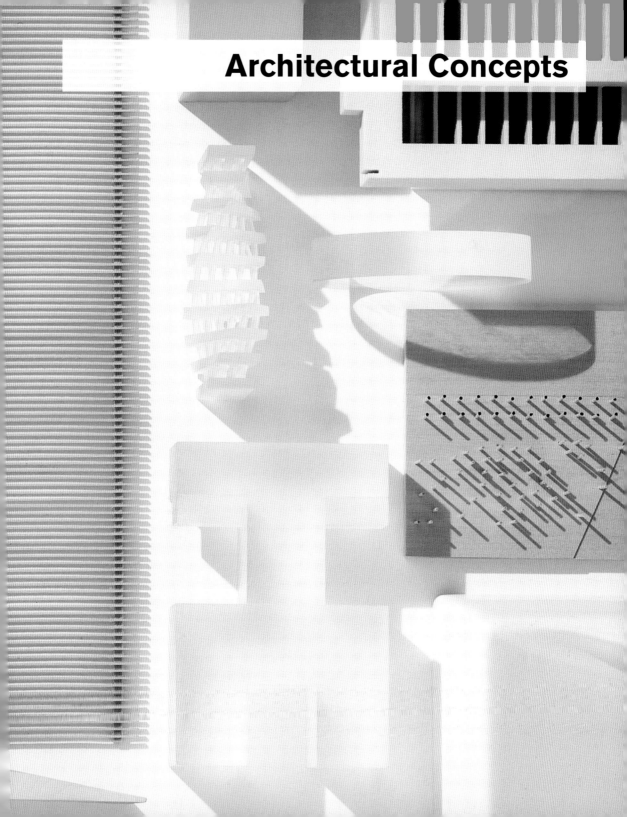

Architectural Concepts

Abstraction
The expression of an intrinsic or essential quality apart from the form of an object.

Active/passive
The state of existence in motion/the state of inert motion.

Additive
Accumulation of substance.

Animation
The process of embedding interest, spirit, motion, or activity into space.

Appearance
Show outward semblance of aspect.

Ascension
Rising, mounting, or sloping upward.

Asymmetrical
Unbalanced spatial composition of parts.

Circulation
Orderly marked movement through space.

Color
A visual attribute of an object in space that results from the light the object emits, transmits, or reflects.

Concave
Curved inward below the plane.

Continuous
Extension in space, time, or sequence without interruption.

Contours
Line on a map connecting points in space of equal height.

Contrast
A difference in visual density.

Converge
Move toward the same point in space.

Convex
Curved outward above the plane.

Core
The body or center of an object.

Dark
Light or hue deficiency.

Density
Spatial concentration.

Depth
Perpendicular measurement downward from a surface.

Detail
An extended treatment of particulars: part of a whole.

Diagonal
Line segment joining two non-adjacent corners of a plane figure or two corners not in the same plane of a solid.

Diagram
Visible mapping of a relationship, abstract concept, or action.

Dimension
X, y, and z coordinates that determine a position in space.

Disintegrate
Loss of integrity by breaking apart.

Edge
The termination of a surface or the joint of two surfaces of a three-dimensional object.

Elevation
The projection of an object or structure onto a vertical plane.

Enclosure
Surround in space.

Envelope
Wrap or cover in space.

Erosion
To diminish gradually.

Exponential
A pattern of change.

Extrusion
Object of fixed cross-sectional profile.

Facade
Face, elevation, or front of a building.

Figure/ground
The perception of difference between foreground
and background.

Film
A thin layer or sheet.

Flexible
Elastic, bending without breaking.

Fluid
Continuous matter subject to change.

Fold
Bend one part over the other.

Form
The configuration of an object as distinguished
from its material.

Fractal
A self-similar, irregular, geometric object that is
repeated at every scale and cannot be represented
with classical geometry.

Frame
A rigid structure or border to enclosure

Geometric
Relative position of figures in space.

Glaze
Fill with glass.

Grade
A step in space.

Gradient
A graded change in magnitude.

Graphic
Visual representation of data.

Grid
A network of horizontal and vertical lines.

Ground
An anchored position.

Haptic
Relationship between space and the sense
of touch.

Hatch
Fine, closely spaced lines.

Hierarchy
An ordered series within a system.

Hue
Gradation of color.

Hybrid
A blend.

Incremental
Small steps over time.

Interaction
Reciprocal action.

Interface
A surface forming a common boundary.

Interpretation
A translation.

Intersecting
Cross at a point or share common space.

Inversion
Interchange of position, order, form, or relationship.

Join
Connect.

Juxtaposition
Placing in spatial proximity.

Lamination
Layers of material bonded together.

Landscape
Land forms.

Layer
A thickness of material laid on a surface.

Light
Illumination.

Line
The trace of a moving point.

Linework
Score.

Macro
A large scale.

Map
A diagram of relation or connection.

Massing
Three-dimensional volume that has or gives the illusion of having weight, density, and bulk.

Materiality
The interaction of the qualities of material objects and space.

Matrix
An array of quantities.

Micro
Minute in scope and scale.

Modularity
System in which the individual components are maintained independently from the remainder of the system.

Monochrome
Made in the shade of a single color.

Narrative
Story.

Negative
Removal of something positive.

Oblique
Neither perpendicular nor parallel.

Obstruct
To block view.

Opacity
Visible light obscured.

Organic
Shapes or forms that are irregular in contour and seem to resemble or suggest forms found in nature.

Orientation
Location or position relative to points in space.

Ornamentation
Added detail.

Overlapping
Extend over and cover a portion.

Pattern
An interrelationship of qualities, forms, lines, tendencies, etc., forming a consistent arrangement.

Penetration
To pierce into or through.

Place
A physical space or environment.

Plane
A flat surface.

Platform
A raised horizontal flat surface.

Point
A definite position without extension.

Portal
An entrance.

Positive
Space that is occupied by form.

Progression
A continuous and connected series; a sequence.

Projection
The representation of a figure or solid on a plane viewed from a specific direction.

Proximity
Nearness in place, time, order, or relation.

Radial
Going from the center outward.

Realism
The actual or real, as distinguished from the abstract.

Reflective
The ability of a surface to bounce back light.

Relief
The projection of a figure or part from the plane on which it is formed.

Repetition
Reiteration of the same.

Representation
An image to express.

Reveal
A setback of surface or space.

Revolve
To turn on an axis.

Rhythm
A regularly recurrent quantitative change.

Rotation
The process of rotating on or as if on an axis.

Saturation
Maximum absorption.

Scale
The proportion that a representation of an object bears to the object itself.

Screen
To conceal or shelter.

Sculpt
To carve, model, or produce.

Sequence
A connected series in time.

Shell
A hard rigid covering.

Site
A spatial location.

Slab
A thick plate formed from a single mass.

Smooth
Having a continuous even surface.

Solid
Mass without an internal cavity.

Space

A boundless three-dimensional extent in which objects and events occur and have relative position and direction.

Span

To extend between points.

Stack

An orderly pile.

Static

A lack of movement.

Structure

Elements arranged in a definite pattern of organization.

Subtraction

Deduction.

Surface

The exterior or upper boundary of an object.

Symmetry

Balanced proportions.

Tangential

Meeting a curve or surface in a single point.

Tent

A canopied enclosure.

Texture

Visual or tactile surface characteristics.

Topography

The configuration of a surface, including its relief and the position of its natural and manmade features.

Translate

To change state, form, or appearance.

Translucency

Transmitting and diffusing light so that objects beyond cannot be seen clearly.

Transparency

Transmitting light without appreciable scattering so that bodies lying beyond are seen clearly.

Undulation

A wavy appearance, outline, or form.

Vertical

Perpendicular to the plane of the horizon.

Visibility

The degree of clearness in view.

Void

Containing nothing.

Volume

The amount of space occupied by a three-dimensional object as measured in cubic units.

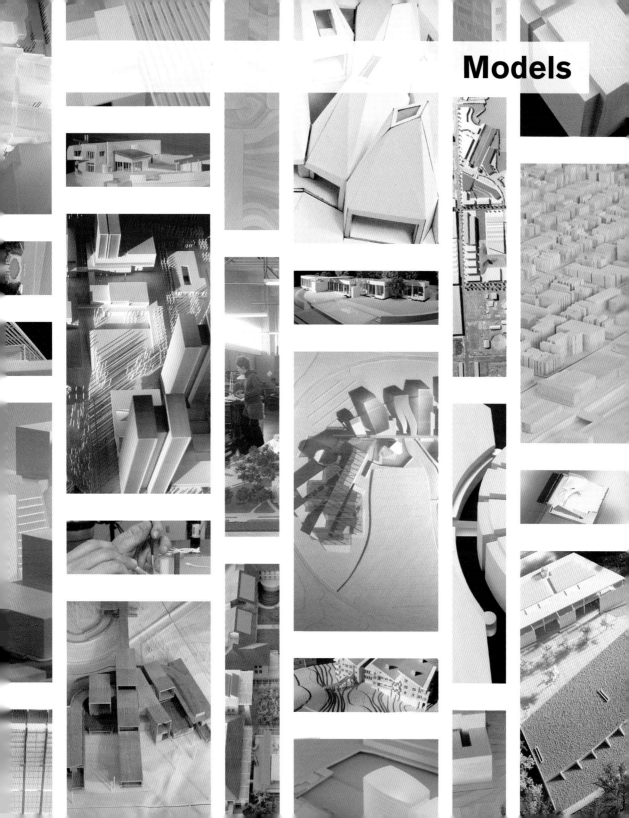

Models

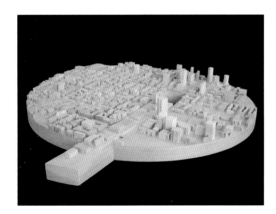

EDAW Inc.

Description: Urban planning study model
Materials: Maple veneer, basswood
Technique: Footprints of buildings were extruded using templates made from model-scale plot.
Scale: 1"=100'-0"

Studios Architecture

Description: Monochromatic presentation model
Materials: Laser-cut and -scored acrylic, metal etch parts
Technique: Components of the model were spray-painted separately to achieve clean crisp edges and to avoid masking transparent areas.
Scale: 1/16"=1'-0"

Gensler

Description: Interior study model
Materials: Gatorboard, mat board, paper
Technique: A lighter ratio of weight to mass was achieved by sheathing gatorboard with paper.
Scale: 3/16"=1'-0"

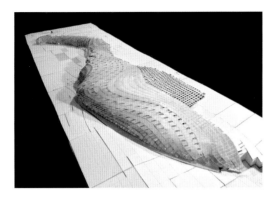

**Brian Osborn, Francis Bitonti, and
Severn Clay-Youman/Pratt Institute**
Description: Study and presentation model
Materials: Museum board, mylar, acrylic
Technique: Mylar was adhered to the structure
to flex and curve as an exterior membrane.
Scale: 1/16"=1'-0"

Lundberg Design
Description: Interior study and exterior
presentation model
Materials: Basswood, foam, acrylic
Technique: Basswood and styrene screen
made by hand
Scale: 1/4"=1'-0"

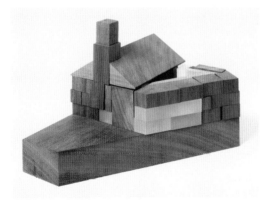

**MOS Architects (Michael Meredith,
Hilary Sample, Mark Talbot, Will MacFarlane,
Jason Bond)**
Description: Massing model
Materials: Wood (mahogany), acrylic solids
Technique: Machined blocks in composite
arrangement
Scale: 1/16"=1'-0"

BAR Architects

Description: Presentation model
Materials: Styrene, acrylic, paint, printed paper
Technique: Stacked acrylic representing glazing
with styrene floor plates
Scale: 1:500 metric

Leddy Maytum Stacy Architects

Description: Museum exhibition model
Materials: Basswood, acrylic, cork, flocking
Technique: Surfaces were flocked to represent
vegetation, built surface texture, and natural
hardscape conditions.
Scale: 1/8"=1'-0"

Lundberg Design
Description: Site model
Materials: Foam, latex shell
Technique: The foam topography was made
with a router (pantograph) using a model scale
plot as a template.
Scale: 3/16"=1'0"

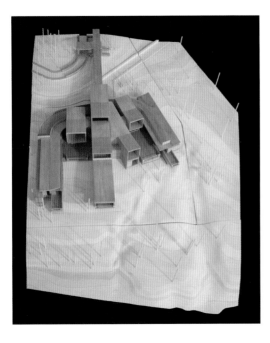

MacCracken Architects
Description: Conceptual presentation model
Materials: Cherry, basswood
Technique: Sanded stacked basswood topography
Scale: 1:100 metric

Quinn Steckel/California College of the Arts
Description: Full-scale study model
Materials: Concrete
Technique: Concrete was cast using a plywood
form mold.
Scale: 1:1 metric

Bade Stageberg Cox
Description: Study and presentation model
Materials: Cardboard, foam board, gesso, glue, paint
Technique: The gessoed or plastered final form was
made from an unfolded pattern generated from a
three-dimensional computer model to determine the
intersections of the curved sections.
Scale: 1/4"=1'-0"

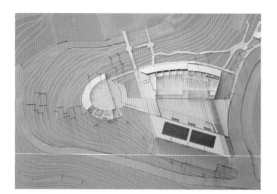

Leddy Maytum Stacy Architects
Description: Study model
Materials: Paper, foam base
Technique: Prints of plan and elevations were
used to mock up a 3-D study.
Scale: 1/16"=1'-0"

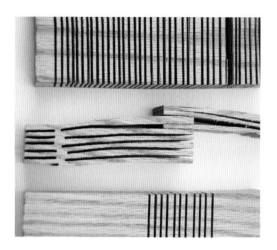

Nicole Powell/California College of the Arts
Description: Material tolerance study
Materials: Wood
Technique: Reveals were cut with a bandsaw.
Scale: 1:1 metric

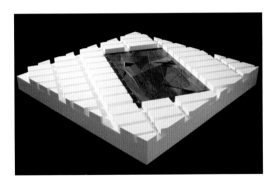

Jeremy Daniel Keagy/Virginia Tech
Description: Urban study model
Materials: Birch plywood, masonite, and matte white paint
Technique: The model was fabricated using the table saw and laser cutting. A CNC could also have routed this surface relief.
Scale: 1/64"=1'-0"

Skidmore, Owings & Merrill
Description: Competition model
Materials: ABS plastic, acrylic
Technique: 3-D print and laser-cut acrylic elements
Scale: 1"=40'-0"

Pfau Architecture
Description: Sectional interior model
Materials: Basswood, metal etch, paint
Technique: Metal-etch elements were painted
to match basswood.
Scale: 1/8"=1'0"

Matthew Bitterman/Virginia Tech
Description: Study model
Materials: Resin, CA cure
Technique: 3-D prints of complex interior elements
Scale: unknown

Lundberg Design
Description: Presentation model
Materials: Basswood, maple, foam, flocking, wire
Technique: The acrylic sheet that represents the pool was sprayed in a color similar to the wood used in the model. The shiny top surface and thickness of the acrylic give it a waterlike appearance.
Scale: 1/4"=1'-0"

Skidmore, Owings & Merrill
Description: Competition model
Materials: Digitally printed mylar, etched stainless steel, metallic paper, Plexiglas
Technique: The graphic information on the facade was digitally printed on mylar.
Scale: 1:200 metric

Archi-tectonics
Description: Exhibition model
Materials: Color acrylic
Technique: Laser-cutting and -scoring color acrylic
Scale: unknown

HOK
Description: Competition model
Materials: Acrylic, styrene
Technique: The sanded acrylic cores capture light, highlighting laser-scored linework.
Scale: 1/16"=1'

J. Mayer H. Architects
Description: Presentation model
Materials: Metal mesh
Technique: A prototype was made out of paper and covered with plaster to form a mold for the metal mesh.
Scale: 1:200 metric

Kohn Pedersen Fox Associates
Description: Presentation model
Materials: Acrylic, metal etch
Technique: Elements of laser-cut and -scored acrylic were painted.
Scale: 1/16"=1'

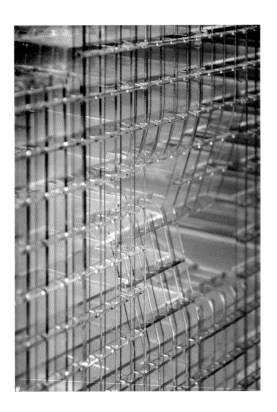

Jason Cross/Rice University
Description: Study model
Materials: Acrylic, wire
Technique: The stacked geometry was
created using 3-D software
Scale: unknown

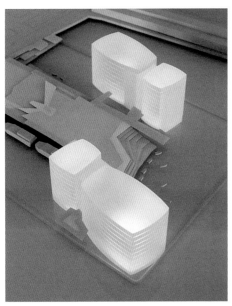

SMWM
Description: Concept presentation model
Materials: Acrylic
Technique: Solid acrylic was hand-scored
and -sanded for light transmission.
Scale: 1:100 metric

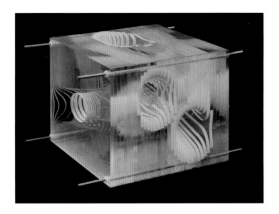

Joyce Hsu/California College of the Arts

Description: Study model

Materials: Acrylic

Technique: Sectional acrylic planes were laser-cut to create interior space.

Scale: Concept model without scale

Lundberg Design

Description: Presentation model

Materials: Cement, aluminum, plywood, brass

Technique: The acrylic roof was heat-bent using a plaster and wood mold.

Scale: 1/2"=1'-0"

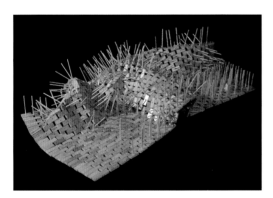

Thomas Whittlesey/ California College of the Arts

Description: Study model

Materials: Pine wood blocks, pine wood dowels, birch plywood, string

Technique: Machine-cut wood elements were strung together to form a flexible plane.

Scale: 1/8"=1'-0"

Leddy Maytum Stacy Architects
Description: Presentation model
Materials: Cork, basswood, metal etch, flocking
Technique: The site was carved out of cork topography.
Scale: 1/16"=1'-0"

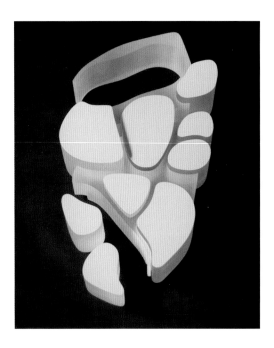

SMWM
Description: Competition model
Materials: Solid acrylic
Technique: Organic acrylic forms were created using plot templates, machined, and hand-sanded.
Scale: 1/16"=1'-0"

Ben Harth/California College of the Arts
Description: Study concept model
Materials: MDF, acrylic tubes
Technique: Acrylic tubes were used to create a pattern.
Scale: unknown

HOK
Description: Massing model
Materials: Cherry, walnut, basswood, acrylic
Technique: Reveals were cut with the table saw to create scale and form.
Scale: 1:100 metric

Bibliography

Abruzzo, Emily, Eric Ellingsen, and Jonathan D. Solomon. *Models: 306090 11*. New York: Princeton Architectural Press, 2008.

Beylerian, George, and Andrew Dent. *Material ConneXion: The Global Resource of New and Innovative Materials for Architects, Artists and Designers*. New York: John Wiley & Sons, 2005.

Hohauser, Sanford. *Architectural and Interior Models*. New York: Van Nostrand Reinhold Company, 1984.

Janke, Rolf. *Architectural Model*s. Translated by Godela V. Xylander. New York: Architectural Book Publishing Co., 1978.

Knoll, Wolfgang, and Martin Hechinger. *Architectural Models: Construction Techniques*. 2nd ed. Fort Lauderdale, FL: J. Ross Publishing, 2007.

Lucci, Roberto, and Paolo Orlandini. *Product Design Models*. New York: Van Nostrand Reinhold, 1990.

McMorrough, Julia. *Materials, Structures, and Standards: All the Details Architects Need to Know but Can Never Find*. Beverly, MA: Rockport Publishers, 2006.

Mills, Criss B. *Designing with Models: A Studio Guide to Making and Using Architectural Design Models*. New York: John Wiley & Sons, 2000.

Moore, Fuller. *Modelbuilder's Notebook: A Guide for Architects, Landscape Architects, and Interior Designers*. New York: McGraw-Hill, 1990.

Morris, Mark. *Models: Architecture and the Miniature*. West Sussex, UK: John Wiley & Sons, 2006.

Oswald, Ansgar. *Architectural Models*. Berlin: Dom Publishers, 2009.

Pattinson, Graham D. *A Guide to Professional Architectural and Industrial Scale Model Building*. Englewood Cliffs, NJ: Prentice-Hall, 1982.

Payne, Darwin R. *Materials and Craft of the Scenic Model*. Carbondale, IL: Southern Illinois University Press, 1976.

Piedmont-Palladino, Susan C. *Tools of the Imagination: Drawing Tools and Technologies from the Eighteenth Century to the Present*. New York: Princeton Architectural Press, 2006.

Porter, Tom, and John Neale. *Architectural Supermodels: Physical Design Simulation*. Oxford, UK: Architectural Press, 2000.

Smith, Albert C. *Architecture Model as Machine: A New View of Models from Antiquity to the Present Day*. Oxford, UK: Architectural Press, 2004.

Sutherland, Martha. *Model Making: A Basic Guide*. New York: W. W. Norton & Co., 1999.

Taylor, John. *Model Building for Architects and Engineers*. New York: McGraw-Hill, 1971.

Credits

Matthew Millman of Matthew Millman Photography:
All photography except where noted below

Dina Dobkin:
Illustrations

Megan Werner, Eric Paulson, Ania Wagner, Tudlik Moerk, and Dina Dobkin:
Block fabrication

Archi-Tectonics:
Sample model (pp. 58, 150)

Bade Stageberg Cox:
Sample model (pp. 40, 146)

Brian Osborn:
Sample model (pp. 24, 143)

Brian Rudko of Professional Models:
Foam topography text and block (pp. 34–35)

Charlie Sheldon of Link Studios:
CNC topography block (p. 47)

California College of Arts:
Sample models (pp. 38, 44, 70, 74, 80, 145, 146, 153, 155)

Doug Finnegan of Insight Design:
Metal etch for the metal etch screen block (p. 51)

Gerald Ratto:
Sample models (pp. 26, 32, 48, 50, 54, 56, 60, 76, 143, 144, 147, 148, 149, 150, 154, 143)

J. Mayer H, Architects:
Sample model (pp. 62, 151)

Jack Pottle:
Sample model (pp. 64, 151)

Jason Cross:
Sample model (pp. 66, 152)

Jeremy Keagy:
Sample model (pp. 46, 147)

MOS:
Sample model (pp. 48, 143)

Ryan Buyssens:
Stereolithography block (pp. 49)

Ryan Hughes:
Sample model (pp. 72, 153)

Wright Yang and Oscar Sandalt of 3Drealize:
3-D print block (p. 53)